Freemas
Hidden
Science

Freemasonry's Hidden Brain Science

Michael Schiavello

Lewis Masonic

First published 2019

ISBN 978 0 85318 565 9

Published by Lewis Masonic Ltd
166 Great North Road, Eaton Socon,
St Neots, Cambridgeshire, PE19 8EH

Printed in England.

Visit the Lewis Masonic website at www.lewismasonic.co.uk

Contents

Contents

Foreword
Prologue
Introduction – A book in two parts ... 11

PART 1 – THE ESOTERIC
Freemasonry's symbolic allegories and hidden brain science

1 – What is Freemasonry? ... 17
2 – Here be dragons ... 23
3 – On what is holy ... 35
4 – All about allegory ... 47
5 – A science of symbols ... 55
6 – Never, never, neverrite ... 59
7 – The Lion of the Tribe of Judah ... 67
8 – Brain science ... 75
9 – A Neuroscientific Approach ... 113
10 – An inside job ... 125
11 – The soul and the spirit ... 133
12 – The doorway to your brain ... 139
13 – Masonic G: your second brain ... 145

PART 2 – THE EXOTERIC
Freemasonry's moral science... for the highest kind of oneness

14 – Want to listen: why you must knock on the door ... 153
15 – A Freemason is ready to... ... 159
16 – All of present Freemasonry ... 165
17 – Take no short cuts ... 171
18 – Manage your time effectively ... 179
19 – Avoid suspicion ... 183
20 – The Golden Rule ... 191
21 – My name is Caution ... 195
22 – Riding the goat ... 199
23 – Understanding the real 47th Proposition of Euclid ... 203
24 – The Past Master ... 211
25 – God and Silence: Consciousness as synonymy ... 221

Footnotes ... 229

Foreword

As a young boy of about ten years, I had no idea what a Masonic lodge was or what Freemasons did. I didn't know anyone who was a Mason. The only thing I knew about Freemasonry was that there was a Masonic building in my home town with a square and compasses over the door and the letter G in the middle. I assumed the 'G' stood for God.

In 1950, I moved to Chicago, Illinois, and took a job in construction. My travels in and around Chicago gave me many views of Masonic Temples all over the city, of which there were many. I'd even heard that Chicago had played home to the tallest building in the world once, The Masonic Temple, which at twenty-one storeys birthed the modern skyscraper until its demolition in 1939. Even though I saw so many Masonic buildings, I never visited any of them to enquire about the purpose of Masonic lodges.

On vacation in my home town of Greenwood, South Carolina years later, I reunited with old chum Tom Wilson. He asked me if I had ever become a Mason, to which I answered 'no'. Tom suggested that I make myself known to my local Masonic lodge. When I returned to Chicago, I took Tom's advice, visited the local lodge and filled out a petition to join. Soon after I received an acceptance.

Thus, began my journey through the Masonic degrees. I received my first degree in January 1969; my second degree in February 1969; and my third degree of Master Mason in March 1969. Two months later I joined both the Scottish Rite and the Shriners. From 1970 to 1986, I went through the Scottish Rite's Chairs of Rose Croix, and in 1980 I became the Worshipful Master of my lodge.

From the very start of my journey some fifty years ago, and continuing today, Masonry has been the most outstanding spiritual experience of my life. It has taught me so much that I would need a book or two to explain it all, but most of all Masonry taught me the love and understanding of all human needs, including the need for affection to be given and received from my fellow man. I have and continue to receive the greatest joy in taking part in the ritual of each degree and learning what every part of the ritual means. I find the work enjoyable and gratifying, and my travels through Masonry continue to be the most invigorating experiences of my life.

I am blessed to know a Brother such as Michael Schiavello, who took his degrees in Australia and later moved to the USA where he became Worshipful Master of Daylite Lodge #44 F&AM in Las Vegas, Nevada in 2015. During his time in the East, Michael proved himself as a great and successful Master, and is one of the most knowledgeable Masonic persons I have ever known.

In putting together this foreword, Michael asked me to explain what Freemasonry means to me. My thoughts and feelings are best communicated in this poem. It was originally a poem by Roy Croft entitled, *I Love You*, and by inserting the word Freemasonry, I feel this poem best tells you just how much the Craft means to me.

I love you Freemasonry
Because you have done
More than any creed
Could have done
To make me good
And more than any fate
Could have done
To make me happy.

Perhaps that's what being a Mason means
after all.

Edward Hall*
PM, 33°

* Edward Hall, 94, lives in Las Vegas, Nevada. He is a Past Master and 33° Mason. Edward is one of the last remaining Pearl Harbor survivors who lived through the horrors of that fateful day, 7 December 1941.

Prologue

For a long time, the knock on Freemasons was that they're in league with the devil. Masters of deception. Illuminati. Puppeteers of the masses.

None of this is true, but as the saying goes, 'rumours are started by haters, spread by fools and accepted by idiots'.

In this case the hater was a man named Leo Taxil, a con artist, writer and practical joker of the 19th century who heaped ridicule on both the Catholic Church and Freemasonry.

Later in his life, Taxil admitted to the giant hoax he perpetuated on the world, stating:

The public made me what I am, the arch-liar of the period, for when I first commenced to write against the Masons my object was amusement pure and simple. The crimes laid at their door were so grotesque, so impossible, so widely exaggerated, I thought everybody would see the joke and give me credit for originating a new line of humour. But my readers wouldn't have it so; they accepted my fables as gospel truth, and the more I lied for the purpose of showing that I lied, the more convinced became they that I was a paragon of veracity.

Even after Taxil's admittance, much of the world, including the Vatican, continued to believe what he had written about Freemasonry was true.

Truth always wins, but liars get their way first. With more research being done into the genuine teachings of Freemasonry and its psychological, psychical and physical benefits, a new generation of young men are joining the Craft and reaping the benefits of a system of self-improvement tried, tested and proven by some of the greatest achievers in history including: Benjamin Franklin, George Washington, Wolfgang Mozart, John Wayne, Henry Ford, Sir Arthur Conan Doyle, Rudyard Kipling, Simon Bolivar, Charles Lindbergh, John Elway, Winston Churchill and Steve Wozniak.

In the following pages you will find examples of the genius of

Freemasonry and uncover the true teachings of the Craft, which run far deeper than moral and social virtues.

If you've ever sat in lodge mouthing the words of the ritual and wondered, 'What am I doing here and how is this benefitting me?' you will find the answers in this book. They may not be the answers presented to you on the pages of your ritual, but they are the answers intended by the ritual writers who, you will discover, were geniuses well ahead of their time.

F. Scott Fitzgerald said: 'Genius is the ability to put into effect what is on your mind.' The writers of Masonic ritual put into effect detailed instructions about the workings of the body, brain, mind and spirit. They were highly intelligent men educated in a variety of subjects in science and philosophy. With no intention of conveying historical accuracy, they wrote to impart vital lessons about the physical, psychological and psychical make-up of a human being. They hid these lessons from the masses, 'veiled in allegory' and 'illustrated by symbols', making them discoverable only to those willing to take up a chisel and gavel, and chip away at the surface.

Seek. Push. Improve. Transcend.

Seek. Push. Improve. Transcend. This is the calling inherent in every man. It is a necessity of the human spirit, no matter the circumstance, opposition, or even understanding. You are a determined creature. You are fearfully and wonderfully made. If you don't think you're as good as you're supposed to be, put your trust in something that can make you better. The will to improve yourself comes from within, not without. Internalise this realisation. You're constantly surrounded by enemies to your personal progression. The key is not to constantly battle your enemies, but to make your position so strong that you're unassailable to your enemies. He who has the higher ground, noble in acts, deeds and thoughts, has the advantage.

Introduction
– a book of two parts

You're about to read a book of two parts. This shouldn't come as a surprise, as the Masonic symbol of the black and white pavement tells us that everything in life is duality.

To have an up, you must have a down. To have cold, you must have warmth. For 'in' to exist, so too must 'out'. And for every positive, there is a negative.

Masonic instruction is dual in nature. Albert Pike calls the division 'exoteric' Freemasonry and 'esoteric' Freemasonry.

The exoteric side of Freemasonry consists of the explanations of the symbols and working tools used in the ritual of the three degrees. This is Pike's 'outer portico of the Temple'.

These symbols and working tools contain moral lessons on how one should live their life. They teach you to live as the best version of yourself, 'an upright man and Mason'. If you adhere to the exoteric lessons of Freemasonry, you cannot help but become a much, much better person.

The esoteric side of Freemasonry is what Pike writes about as the ritual's 'true explication' reserved for the 'Adepts, the Princes of Masonry'.

These Adepts and Princes aren't, of course, actual princes. The prince is you. If you're willing to dig beneath the words of the ritual, and truly examine the depths of Freemasonry's esoteric teachings, you're a prince on his way to becoming a king, for as Proverbs tells us: 'It is God's glory to conceal a thing and the king's glory to discover it.'

Are you ready to become a king?

Esoteric isn't bad
The word 'esoteric' gets a bad rap these days. In fact, most people don't understand what 'esoteric' means.

As defined at dictionary.com: *esoteric – understood by or meant for only the select few who have special knowledge or interest.*

In purchasing this book, you have shown special interest in the Science of Freemasonry. The esoteric teachings of the Craft as well as the exoteric teachings are now in your hands. How far you want to go down the rabbit's hole is up to you.

Esoteric Freemasonry, that is, Freemasonry beyond the limited descriptions of the working tools, symbols, and allegories, is not for everyone. And that's fine! Freemasonry is something different to each of us.

If you want to go deep, go deep.

If you want to remain in the 'outer portico' of the body of knowledge, that's okay.

You get out of Freemasonry as much as you choose to put in.

The exoteric portion of this book deals with the application of Freemasonry in everyday life. I will talk about that with which we are all familiar: the plumb line, the Golden Rule, the Winding Staircase, riding the goat, avoiding suspicion, the 24-inch gauge, caution, and much more.

The esoteric portion of this book deals with a discovery I made while plumbing the depths of Masonic ritual and symbolism. It is the discovery of Freemasonry's hidden Brain Science.

I will prove that Freemasonry is a metaphysical and neurological handbook detailing how to raise your higher consciousness from your lower self, centred around the brain and the mind.

I will provide you with jaw-dropping facts that prove the Masonic ritual writers of centuries ago veiled in allegory the science of the brain and its workings for us Adepts and Princes to discover.

The ritual writers were geniuses, of this there is no doubt. In the Legend of the Third Degree they wrote a story about what happens inside the body when certain activities are practised that put into motion electrical charges that affect the brain in a positive manner.

Like all mythologists, the Masonic ritual writers veiled their lessons in the dramatisation of a story so that in time evolved minds could decode its true, hidden meaning.

The story of Hiram Abiff's death and raising is a myth with neurological and metaphysical lessons, like other myths such as the twelve Labours of Hercules; David and Goliath; Jonah in the belly of the sea creature; Samson and Delilah; the Epic of Gilgamesh; the legend of King Arthur; Pandora's Box; the journeys of Ulysses; the lost city of Atlantis; Adam and Eve in the Garden of Eden; even Indiana Jones and his search for the lost ark.

As Joseph Campbell said: 'Myths are clues to the spiritual potentialities of the human life.'

The true purpose of Freemasonry, as you will see, is to re-energise the body, the glands, the nerve centres, the brain, and the mind so to reignite the dormant pineal gland – your inner spiritual aspect – and reconnect with your divine spark.

The characters we meet in Masonic ritual, the symbols, the working tools, and the lectures are signposts directing you to the potentialities of your consciousness.

You will never find the bones of Hiram Abiff for he never lived as a real person.

You will never see a fragment of the pillars Boaz and Jachin in a museum as they never stood at the entrance of a real Temple.

You will never find a record of the workmen of the Temple, for there were no actual workmen.

However, you will discover what Hiram Abiff represents.

You will uncover the true secrets placed in the hollow centre of the pillars Boaz and Jachin.

And you will realise that King Solomon's true Temple is your self, specifically your brain.

In my lectures during my time as Worshipful Master of Daylite #44 F&AM in Las Vegas, Nevada, I often spoke about my belief that Freemasonry holds all the answers to all the questions about who we are, why we are, where we are and where we are going. Not when read in the literal sense, but when read from a sense of identifying the clues, searching them out, and discovering the hidden truths concealed beneath its words and symbols.

Writes Albert Pike:

> It is for each individual Mason to discover the secret of Masonry, by reflection upon its symbols and a wise consideration and analysis of what is said and done in the work. Masonry does not inculcate her truths. She states them, once and briefly; or hints them, perhaps, darkly; or interposes a cloud between them and eyes that would be dazzled by them. "Seek, and ye shall find, knowledge and truth."[1]

Freemasonry will never present its hidden teachings on a silver platter. Like a treasure map, you are provided with the symbols, the signposts, the prompts and clues, and must do the groundwork yourself.

Turn the page now.

Unfold the treasure map.

Let me lead you to the symbolic 'X' where we will discover the hidden treasures of Freemasonry together.

PART 1

THE ESOTERIC
Freemasonry's symbols, allegories, and hidden brain science

– 1 –
What is Freemasonry?

'What is Freemasonry?' is a question many Freemasons find difficult to answer. It shouldn't be. If you can't answer concisely to what Freemasonry is, you're most likely not understanding the work. And Freemasonry *is* work; the most important work, as you will discover in the following pages.

Freemasonry is many things to many people. It is a craft, an art, a science, a curriculum, a fraternity, a philosophy, and as much or as little as you want it to be. But even this description is not an accurate or adequate answer as to what Freemasonry is.

Above all else, Freemasonry is a system of self-improvement. It has to be. Without self-improvement as both the journey and the destination, Freemasonry is pointless. Practising Freemasonry without the ambition of self-improvement renders useless its symbols, allegories, rituals and regalia.

Millions of men over hundreds of years have reaped the rewards of the progressive science of Freemasonry.

For centuries the Craft has provided a map for men to follow on their path to personal betterment. Freemasonry is a time-tested system of teaching rooted in the mystery schools of Ancient Egypt, infused with the ideas of the great Greek philosophers, impressed with lessons communicated by teachers before the Common Era (BCE), through to the Renaissance and still relevant today. To knock on the door of Freemasonry and partake of its rituals and oaths is a commitment by an individual to pursue a time-tested and effective system of instruction for improving himself in mind, body and spirit.

Freemasonry is an external method of improving the internal part of oneself remembering, as ritual tells us, *it is the internal not the external qualifications of a man that Freemasonry regards.* It is a method of unlocking the doorways that allow you to discover your enormous potential.

Internalisation takes place when something you know becomes

something you believe in and live by. You can read words and attain knowledge, but only when knowledge is applied is wisdom attained.

The symbols of Freemasonry are the embodiment of ideas emanating from a higher plane. When applied to internal use, they serve to smooth your rough ashlar, raise your consciousness and reveal the divine spark at your centre, thus purging your lower nature to manifest your higher consciousness, your connection to Supreme Consciousness – your true self.

As I've stated many times in my lodge lectures, if a man follows the teachings of Freemasonry, internalises these teachings, and adheres to the lessons detailed in the ritual, he cannot possibly err in life. Within the pages of our little ritual books given us after completion of the third degree are lessons written by geniuses which, if internalised, will keep you on the right side of life's tracks without any possibility of wandering off.

It's fiction. That's a fact!

What makes Freemasonry a unique system of self-improvement is its method of teaching through allegory and symbolism.

What is allegory?

An allegory is an extended metaphor. The story's elements – location, objects, plot points, characters – are beyond literal. They represent something much deeper than the simplicity of the story itself.

The 'historic' stories in the Masonic degrees are all allegorical. From the building of King Solomon's Temple to the death of Grand Master Hiram Abiff, the three ruffians, the seafaring man, and the death of the Ephraimites on the banks of the River Jordan, none of these events ever actually happened. They're allegorical funnels designed for the flow-through of Freemasonry's timeless lessons.

Masonic working tools, symbols and allegories contain powerful metaphysical messages couched in fascinating stories that make for incredible reading and drama. They are written in such a way as to imprint these messages on your mind. In other words, they're written in a way as to not be forgotten.

Digging beneath the surface

History's most unforgettable stories contain messages that run much deeper than literary entertainment.

George Orwell's *Animal Farm* is, on the surface, a story about farm animals. Beneath the surface, it is an allegorical depiction of the political situation in Stalin's Russia.

Yann Martel's *Life of Pi* is the story of a boy who grows up in a zoo and later becomes trapped on a boat with a tiger in the middle of the ocean. What it's really about, however, is a young man of multiple faiths and his relationship with God (symbolised by the tiger).

In the film *Groundhog Day*, Phil Connors lives the same day over and over again. The film is an allegory for the path to enlightenment. Phil is stuck in a state of purgatory. Only after performing selfless deeds does he finally transcend his animal self (his selfish, egotistical, brute nature) and prove his true, greatest self to a higher power, thus freeing him from the cycle.

The Bible is full of allegories and parables (simple stories used to convey spiritual messages). These include:

Adam and Eve in the garden of Eden
Jonah in the belly of the giant sea creature
David versus Goliath
Samson and Delilah
Daniel in the lion's den
Moses parting the Red Sea
Noah's Ark
The prodigal son's return
None of them actually happened.

These stories stand the test of time and translate into fantastic Hollywood drama, but they never actually took place. How do I know this? Because the Bible writers tell me so.

Paul tells us that the story of Isaac, Ishmael, Hagar and Sara is not factual but allegorical. Galatians 4:24: 'Which things are an allegory.'

Matthew tells us that Jesus spoke in parables only: 'All these things spoke Jesus unto the multitudes in parables, and without a parable spake he not unto them.'

And how about the Psalmist who wrote: 'I will open my mouth in a parable: I will utter dark sayings of old.'

The Bible writers refer to the ancient teachings as 'dark sayings' because they're hidden from the masses. One must dig beneath the surface to uncover their real meaning. A haircut never reduced Samson's strength; a burning bush didn't talk to Moses; and Noah never ushered two of every creature into a wooden ark. Through meditation, contemplation and introspection, you're supposed to bring to light the true meanings of the 'dark sayings.'

It's your choice

If you choose to believe that a man survived in the stomach of a giant sea creature for three days and then got spewed up onto a beach, you choose to miss the lesson beneath the surface in the story of Jonah. Such lessons are always concealed from those unwilling to search them out. But search them out you must, for as Proverbs 25:2 tells us: 'It is the glory of God to conceal a thing, but it's the glory of a king to discover it.'

You're the king! All that is concealed awaits your discovery. A secret is only secret until it's found out. The ancient mystery schools worked this way, and it is from these mystery schools that Freemasonry developed.

If you choose to believe that the structural information on the building of King Solomon's Temple is an accurate, historic account, you choose to miss uncovering the real 'secrets' of Freemasonry.

In the following pages you will discover that Masonic ritual was written by true geniuses to relay instructions about the workings of your body, brain, mind and spirit.

What's the point?

There has to be a deeper message in Solomon's Temple beyond mere facts and stats about a building.

Why tell us that the timber was felled and prepared in the forests of Lebanon?

Why do we care that the timber was conveyed by sea in floats to Joppa?

Why inform us that the pillars were cast in the clay grounds on the banks of the River Jordan between Succoth and Zeredatha?

What does it matter that the pillars were hollow?

And why did it take seven years for exactly 153,303 men to construct a building that was little larger in floor size than a tennis court?

How is this even believable?

By modern comparison, it took 12,000 workers six years to build the Burj Khalifa in Dubai, the world's tallest building.

Clearly, we are not meant to take the Masonic story of the building of King Solomon's Temple on face value. Beneath the surface are lessons in neuroscience and metaphysical lessons about our own physical, mental and spiritual make up.

If you're willing to peel the layers of the onion, to pierce the veil, and to seek light, more light, and further light in this tried and tested system of self-improvement, the most wonderful rewards await you.

Still don't believe me?

Do you still believe Masonic ritual and lectures are not about the functioning of your body, your brain, your mind and your divine spark?

Let me present something else to you, more of which will be explained later on.

King Solomon's Temple isn't an actual building. It's you! Every piece of the temple as described in the Masonic lectures is a representation of you.

Freemasonry is very much about your brain. Beneath the surface it tells us about how your brain works, how to align your brain with your body and use both to raise your consciousness and ignite your divine spark.

Try this on for size.

We're told that the two pillars which stood at the entrance of King Solomon's Temple, named Boaz and Jachin, measured *18 cubits high*. The human spinal cord, which extends from the brain to the lumbar region, is *18 inches high*.

Each pillar was topped with chapiters of *5 cubits* each. The human brain is *5 inches* wide.

Boaz and Jachin were hollow pillars with a *circumference of 12 cubits*. The human spinal cord is hollow with *a circumference of 12mm*.[2]

The chapiters (symbolic of the human brain) were decorated with lily work. Lily flowers open at the top like a trumpet. In Eastern religion it is the opened lotus flower that represents the awakened individual.

The pillars Boaz and Jachin symbolise your end goal: to be brought to light!

What is the *only* thing a Freemason ever asks for in any of the Masonic degrees?

Light!

It's all about awakening and illumination. This was the end goal for mystery school initiates, just as it should be the end goal for the modern Freemason. Freemasonry is built upon the traditions of the universal science and philosophy taught in the mystery schools of ancient Egypt, Persia, India, Chaldea and Greece. Every word and movement of Masonic ritual serves as a living monument to the mystery schools of the past whose goal was the realisation of a state of consciousness greater than presently exhibited, contained in a state of potential.

Illumination awaits

Freemasonry is a user's manual describing the proper function and potential of the human being. Through a proven system of progressive science, the individual is awakened to his higher self – to the optimum functioning of his brain, body, mind and spirit – for the illumination of his divine spark.

Masonic allegories were penned by masters. They were geniuses in the subjects of biology, psychology and physiology, astronomy, astrology, and anthropology, standing high above the greatest scientific minds of our modern age. They didn't write for historical accuracy, they wrote to impart important lessons about the workings of the body, brain, mind and spirit. They were ahead of their time.

The Realm of Geniuses

Californian Freemason Thomas Burnett PM, a former civil and structural engineer with a deep interest in astronomy and geometry, first alerted me to a piece of Masonic ritual that points directly to the genius of its writers.

Take this excerpt from the Middle Chamber lecture: 'Numberless worlds are around us, all framed by the same Divine Artist, which roll through the vast expanse, and are all conducted by the same unerring law of Nature.'

It wasn't until the early 1920s that astronomer Edwin Hubble provided proof that our Milky Way was just one small part of a staggeringly vast universe.

The Middle Chamber lecture, from the Preston-Webb work written in the 1800s, shows that Masonic writers were aware of the *numberless worlds around us* well before Hubble!

They knew that these worlds *roll* through the universe, that is, the stars, the planets, and all other bodies in space are in constant motion. The universe isn't static!

Hubble is also credited with the discovery of the expanding universe in 1929, later confirmed by Einstein's equations. But the geniuses who penned Masonic ritual knew of the expanding universe well before Hubble.

Thanks to Hubble, we now know that the universe is expanding (short explanation – due to Dark Energy) and the space between all galaxies is growing larger every second. Hubble's discovery has been verified and the expansion acceleration has been measured by astronomers using the telescope that bears his name. The current value for the Hubble constant, which is being verified by more and more accurate measurements, is approximately 72km/sec per megaparsec.

Masonic writers knew of the expanding universe more than 200 years ago! That's why they wrote of the planets and stars *which roll through the vast expanse,* the definition of expanse being: 'the distance to which something expands or can be expanded'.

Astrophysicist and science writer John Gribbin wrote that: 'The discovery of the century, in cosmology at least, was without doubt the dramatic discovery made by Hubble, and confirmed by Einstein's equations that the Universe is not eternal, static, and unchanging.'

Freemasonry, however, taught these facts well before Hubble was said to have discovered them!

Why does all this matter?
It's important for you to know that when it comes to Masonic ritual and lectures, you are learning from the realm of geniuses. Men so intelligent that they concealed great moral, social, physical and psychical lessons which are only discoverable to those willing to look beneath the surface.

Masonic ritual contains all the lessons a man needs to live a noble life of purpose, and to groom him for life beyond the physical. Freemasonry is a progressive science for the enhancement of your non-physical self. One who adheres strictly to the science cannot possibly err in his moral make up.

Freemasonry really does make good men better.

Masonic ritual is part life lessons, part neurological handbook, part psychological training manual, part metaphysical guide telling you:

Who you are;
What you are;
How you are;
Why you are;
What you can be.

More than morals
When asked what Freemasonry teaches, a common answer is, 'It teaches morals'.

While Freemasonry does seek to develop a man's moral conscience, we must admit that treating everyone equally, living an upright life, and the value of an education are things a child understands. We don't need levels, plumb rules and chisels to remind us to be good people.

If you choose to believe that such simple moral lessons are all Freemasonry teaches, you choose to swim in the shallow end. Stay there if you like, but if you care to venture into the depths of the knowledge pool, read on.

Freemasonry is an interior work. It is the internal not the external qualifications of a man that Freemasonry regards. As with any other discipline which guides the student in interior work, the objective of Freemasonry is to ignite the candidate's divine spark, that is to raise his lower consciousness to higher consciousness and connect with the presence of Divinity within himself; Supreme Consciousness.

Masonic author W. Kirk MacNulty writes that the teachings of Freemasonry derive from the Renaissance period. 'After considering what evidence is available, most serious historians (Masons and non-Masons alike) who have examined the subject consider that the Order evolved in the late 1500s or early 1600s that is, towards the end of the English Renaissance.'[3]

The essential belief of the Renaissance scholar, writes MacNulty, is that 'the individual human being could turn within himself, rise up through the "celestial world of the soul" (psyche) and the "super celestial world of the Spirit", and perceive the presence of God within himself.'[4] While modern psychology is focused on life in contemporary society and the physical world, MacNulty writes that the Renaissance scholar 'considered the psyche to be a bridge between the physical world and the world of the Spirit.'

Freemasonry teaches one to integrate the bicameral mind (think Boaz and Jachin) into a state of balanced consciousness (walking between the two pillars), leading to a state of higher consciousness.

'Freemasonry is the custodian of a symbolism which contains, at the same time, a model of the psyche and rituals which have been designed to have specific effects on the candidate at the psychological level', writes MacNulty.[5]

The characters you meet along the way, the dramas acted out, the working tools employed, and the symbols depicted, are universal teachings to the potential of human consciousness and experiences applicable to everyone.

Why are you here?
Inside you is a master.

He is the best of you; your higher consciousness.

It is your job to find him, grab hold of him and raise him.

It is said that when the student is ready, the teacher appears.

Are you ready?

In the following pages I will delve into the deeper aspects of Masonic symbolism, and how such symbols build a man's character, a result of which is the enhancement of the spirit.

I will also delve into the allegory of King Solomon's Temple, its construction, the materials used, and the characters behind its construction, namely King Solomon of Israel, King Hiram of Tyre, the three ruffians Jubelo, Jubela and Jubelum, and Hiram Abiff, his death and burial. You will come to realise that behind this timeless story is a deep message about who you are and what you can be.

You may not accept everything you read in this book, and that's fine. Many Freemasons wish to float on the surface of the Royal Art, amongst the pageantry, the festive boards, and the lectures on morals and good will. I'm not condemning such an approach to Freemasonry.

If you want to go deeper and uncover what the genius ritual writers hid from all but those willing to get their hands dirty, then let's go on an adventure together through the Masonic wonderland, always remembering: 'It is the glory of God to conceal a thing, but it's the glory of a king to discover it.'

– 2 –
Here be dragons

Is there really a hidden meaning in Masonic ritual? The answer is a definitive 'yes.' In fact, the ritual itself tells us more than once that its true teachings are hidden from plain sight, and Masonic authors have long written and hinted about Freemasonry's concealed lessons.

In his book *Freemasonry – Its Hidden Meaning,* George H. Steinmetz writes: 'The average Mason is lamentably ignorant of the real meaning of the Masonic Symbology and knows little of its esoteric teaching.'

The word 'esoteric' derives from the Greek *esoterikos,* derived from *esotero,* meaning 'within'. Lucian first ascribed the word to Aristotle who had inner (esoteric) and outer (exoteric) teachings, and later came to designate the secret doctrines of Pythagoras who taught to a select group of students (disciples). Defined simply, what is esoteric is hidden from outsiders, non-public, usually associated with secret or semi-secret spiritual teachings.

Esotericism bears a close affinity with mysticism.

Mysticism comes from the Greek adjective *mystikos* which is used to denote anything connected with the mysteries. A mystic is one who passed through the rituals of initiation, or mysterion – a mystery or secret initiation – in order to understand the ultimate reality, which is a transcendence of common reality (the physical perception) to a higher reality. A mystic believes there is a deeper state of existence beyond the daily grind of the material world. He relies on direct experience, not on indirect knowledge or theory, to attain union with ultimate reality.

Mysticism and esotericism
Freemasonry is both a mystic and esoteric pursuit, and it's easy to see how the two words have become routinely interchangeable. One who has undergone Masonic initiation is a mystic and is then open to pursue the esoteric teachings of the Craft. Initiation alone will not lead one to union with ultimate reality; this is the realm of esoteric knowledge. This is why, as Steinmetz writes, to know little of Freemasonry's esoteric teaching is indeed lamentable.

Brother Robert G. Davis in his essay, *The Path of Esotericists Among Us,*[6] states that 'we all know Masons who believe with all their heart that there is nothing spiritual about the rituals of Masonry. There are those who claim there is nothing to learn beyond the ritual words'.

Such a belief simply isn't true, as will attest anyone who has read Masonic authors such as Pike, Wilmshurst, Steinmetz, Mackey, and more recently Robert Lomas.

Beyond the writings of these authors, and the words found in this book, the onus is on you and you alone to delve into the hidden aspects of the Craft and uncover its treasures. The choice is yours. A swimming pool is one body of water with two ends, shallow and deep. Both are indiscernible to the naked eye and only experienced through jumping into the water. The same could be said of Freemasonry.

In *Morals and Dogma,* Albert Pike writes:

> *The Blue Degrees are but the court or outer portico of the Temple. Part of the symbols are displayed there to the initiate, but he is intentionally misled by false interpretations. It is not intended that he shall understand them; but it is intended that he shall imagine that he understands them...their true explication is reserved for the Adepts, the Princes of Masonry.*

Giovani Giacomo Casanova in his *Memoirs, Volume 2a,* notes that:

> *Those who stop at the outward crust of things imagine that the secret consists in words, in signs, or that the main point of it is to be found only in reaching the highest degree. This is a mistaken view: the man who guesses the secret of Freemasonry, and to know it you must guess it, reaches that point only through long attendance in the lodges, through deep thinking, comparison, and deduction.*

Philosopher Benedict Spinoza writes in *Ethics:* 'All noble things are as difficult as they are rare,' which applies to the teachings of Freemasonry. There is no nobler pursuit than self-improvement, and doing so through any means, particularly through the degrees of Freemasonry, is no easy task. To dig beneath the surface, follow the clues and signposts, detach from superstition and dogma, and use reason and logic to unearth the hidden secrets of Freemasonry is an adventure only undertaken by the brave and determined. It is in the esoteric, hidden from plain sight, that the true teachings of Freemasonry are found. It is here, behind the symbols, deeper than the words of the ritual, that knowledge awaits discovery; knowledge deeper than morals and social virtues, which are taught to every child, and for which Freemasonry is not necessary.

Most, however, choose to remain strictly in chartered territory, never venturing beyond the common boundaries, to that part of the Masonic treasure map where it is written, 'Here be dragons'.

Beyond chartered territory

'Here be dragons' was a phrase frequently used in the 1700s and earlier by cartographers on distant corners of their maps to indicate the end of the known world. With no explanation as to what lay past the known boundaries of their existence, the map makers simply wrote, 'Here be dragons', as a means of deterring those bold adventurers seeking to go beyond the borders known to the masses. In other words, to go beyond the edge, to live in search of the meaning and mysticism that accompany adventures into the unknown, one had to be willing to step foot in a place where most would dare not go.

If designated the role of Masonic cartographer, most Freemasons would be quick to write the words 'Here be dragons', at any mention of Freemasonry's hidden teachings. Lacking the ambition and determination to venture past the words on the pages of the ritual, thinking them merely moral lessons and as such the be-all-and-end-all of Masonic teaching, they deny themselves the treasure that lies beyond Pike's outer portico. But there *are* hidden mysteries in Freemasonry, and by the very definition of hidden one must be willing to find these mysteries to attain the true teachings of the Masonic system. As Robert V. Lund writes in his article 'Evidence of a Hidden Meaning in Masonic Ritual' on the website www.freemasoninformation.com: 'Our ritual hides deeper, more esoteric, *spiritual* lessons, based on various *ancient mysteries and teachings* that have been taught throughout the ages, in different forms, and is still being taught today.'

The ritual tells us so

How do we know that our ritual hides esoteric lessons based on various ancient mysteries and teachings? Because the ritual tells us so.

That our teachings are ancient is undeniable. The candidate for Freemasonry is instructed to enter the lodge and be received in due and *ancient* form. In the Charge at Raising we are told, 'Our *ancient* landmarks you are carefully to preserve.'

The teachings of Freemasonry are mysterious. Candidates for initiation enter upon the path of mysticism.

In the preparation room, the candidate is asked (by the Secretary): 'Do you seriously declare, upon your honour, that unbiased by the improper solicitation of friend, and uninfluenced by mercenary motives, you freely and voluntarily offer yourself a candidate for the *mysteries* of Freemasonry?'

Mysteries are what the candidate is about to discover, the definition of a mystery being: *the practices, skills, or lore peculiar to a particular trade or activity and regarded as baffling to those without specialised knowledge; secrecy or obscurity.*

Later in the initiation ceremony, the candidate obligates that he will 'always hele, forever conceal, and never reveal any of the *secret* arts, parts, or points of the *hidden mysteries* of Freemasonry, which I have received...'

In the Entered Apprentice Charge, the newly made Mason is told to 'keep sacred and inviolate *the mysteries of the Order*, as these are to distinguish you from the rest of the community and mark your consequence among Masons.'

In the presentation of the Three Precious Jewels in the Fellowcraft degree he is told: '...the *mysteries* of Freemasonry are safely lodged in the repository of Faithful Breasts.'

The Charge at Raising begins with these words to the newly raised Master Mason: 'My Brother, your zeal for our Institution, the progress you have made in our *mysteries*, and your steady conformity to our useful regulations, have pointed you out as a proper object for this peculiar mark of our favour.'

Preston's explanation

William Preston is one of Freemasonry's most influential figures. Born in Edinburgh, Scotland in 1742, he was a distinguished instructor of Masonic Ritual and founder of a system of Masonic lectures which still retain their influence.

From 1765 to 1772, Preston engaged in research and correspondence with Freemasons at home and abroad, endeavouring to learn all he could about Freemasonry and the arts it encouraged. These efforts bore fruit in the form of his first book, entitled *Illustrations of Masonry*, published in 1772. He took the old lectures and work of Freemasonry, revised them and placed them in such form as to receive the approval of the leading members of the Craft. Encouraged by their favourable reception and sanctioned by the Grand Lodge, Preston employed, at his own expense, lecturers to travel throughout the kingdom and place the lectures before the lodges. New editions of his book were demanded, and up to the present time it has gone through more than twenty editions in England, six in America, and several more in various European languages.

Writes Preston of Freemasonry's method of teaching via allegory and symbol:

> *Everything that strikes the eye, more immediately engages the attention, and imprints on the memory serious and solemn truths. Masons have, therefore, universally adopted the plan of inculcating the tenets of their Order by typical figures and allegorical emblems, to prevent their mysteries from descending within the familiar reach of inattentive and unprepared novices from whom they might not receive due veneration.*

Preston next explains where the method of such instruction comes from.

> *The usages and customs of Masons have ever corresponded with those of the ancient Egyptians; to which, indeed, they bear a near affinity. Those philosophers, unwilling to expose their mysteries to vulgar eyes, concealed their particular tenets and principles of polity and philosophy under hieroglyphical figures; and expressed their notion of government by signs and symbols which they communicated to their Magi alone, who were bound by oath never to reveal them. Pythagoras seems to have established his system on a similar plan; and many Orders of a more recent date have copied the example.*

We the flag bearers

Mystery schools of the ancient world, including those in India, Chaldea, Egypt and Greece, used a training method of dramatic enactments, allegories and symbols, which taught the origin of things, the nature of the human spirit, its relation to the physical, the methods of purifying the spirit and reconnection to a higher consciousness.

In the above excerpt from *Illustrations of Masonry*, Preston tells us that Freemasonry is the modern flag bearer of the ancient mystery schools. At its hidden core awaiting discovery by those ambitious and determined enough to go beyond the words on the pages of their monitors,

Freemasonry's fundamental tenet, as was that of the true mystery schools who taught the Secret Doctrine or Ancient Wisdom, is the spiritual evolution of the inner being.

If we are to discover Freemasonry's true teachings and reap the rewards of this ancient knowledge of interior work, we need to go beyond the borders, to the place where dragons be.

— 3 —
Un-weird science

What qualifies Freemasonry as a science? And what branch of science do Freemasons practice?

The Fellowcraft degree informs us that Freemasonry is a progressive science thus explained: 'When you were made an Entered Apprentice you were placed at the North East part of the Lodge to show that you were newly admitted; you are now placed at the South East part to mark the progress you have made in the science.'

The pursuit of knowledge is never static. This alone qualifies science as a progressive practice. The word 'pursuit' indicates progress towards the attainment of a goal, and that goal in Freemasonry is the attainment of light. Not light from a bulb or the sun, but the light of knowledge, of which the ability to know thyself is the greatest attainment.

The process of attaining self-knowledge, getting to know who we are, why we are, where we are and where we can go, engages us in the practice of progressive science.

No place for superstition
Unscientific thought and superstition hold no place in Freemasonry. The Craft has always been an advocate of scientific thought. Masons are exhorted to do research into the hidden mysteries of nature and science, with the Old Charges placing emphasis on study of the Seven Liberal Arts and Sciences, being:

Grammar
Rhetoric
Logic
Arithmetic
Geometry
Music
Astronomy

The Seven Liberal Arts and Sciences should always be listed in this manner, beginning with Grammar and ending in Astronomy.

Without first learning Grammar (the art of using words) we cannot practice Rhetoric (speaking and writing to persuade others, adding force and elegance to our thoughts by being thoroughly acquainted with a subject). Both Grammar and Rhetoric are necessary for Logic, which is the art of reasoning that seeks to confront and contrast ideas, identify which is correct and which is not, remove ambiguity, and measure, compare, analyse, prove, and demonstrate facts with clarity.

One can only reason a discussion when thoroughly acquainted with a topic (Rhetoric). Both Rhetoric and Logic are impossible without an understanding of Grammar.

Hence, we see the progressive scientific method that lays a solid foundation in one subject before moving to the next.

The whole of the Trivium (Grammar, Rhetoric, Logic) is dedicated to the cultivation of Language. Grammar is the mechanics of a language; Rhetoric is the use of language to instruct and persuade; Logic is the mechanics of thinking clearly, of comparison and analysis. These three simpler arts enable you to (later) master four complex sciences, the Quadrivium: Arithmetic, Geometry, Music, Astronomy.[7]

Likewise, the Entered Apprentice degree must precede the Fellowcraft degree, and the Master Mason degree follows the Fellowcraft degree. Attainment of appendant body degrees such as the Holy Royal Arch (York Rite) and Sublime Prince of the Royal Secret (Scottish Rite) are only possible after the completion of the preceding degrees in order.

Similarly, ascension through the Chairs of a lodge, from Junior Steward to Worshipful Master, is a process one should undertake without 'jumping' offices. A newly installed Junior Steward, even though he may boast fifty years of Masonic experience, is not qualified to become Worshipful Master the following year. He must go through the chairs and learn the lessons pursuant to each office to prepare himself for a seat in the Oriental Chair.

Advancement in Masonic degrees and through the offices of the lodge represent the 'progressive science' of Freemasonry.

The Royal Society

The history of modern Freemasonry is intimately connected to the Royal Society, a Fellowship of many of the world's most eminent scientists and the oldest scientific academy in continuous existence.

Historians including Margaret Jacob contend that Freemasonry played an important role in European Enlightenment scientific education.

As an interesting side note, I believe that one of the answers to a question asked in the opening of a lodge refers directly to the relationship between Freemasonry and the Royal Society.

In the ritual of opening a lodge, the Worshipful Master asks the following of the Senior Warden:

WM: Are you a Mason?

SW: I am so taken and accepted among Brethren and <u>Fellows</u>.

'Among Brethren' should be the only acknowledgement of his Masonic affiliation the Senior Warden is required to give. His inclusion of the word 'Fellows' suggests that during the late Renaissance, from whence we derive much of our Masonic ritual, being identified by those highly regarded in the scientific community (Fellows of the Royal Society) carried lofty social and intellectual attachment.

The origins of the Royal Society trace to an 'invisible college' of philosophers and scientists who began meeting in the mid-1640s to discuss the ideas of Francis Bacon. Two of the original members – Sir Robert Moray and Elias Ashmole – were already Freemasons at the formation of the Royal Society. The Society met weekly to witness experiments and discuss what would now be called scientific topics although science then was much more broadly defined and included subjects such as alchemy and astrology.

The early years of the Society saw revolutionary advancements in the conduct and communication of science and featured the work of many Freemasons including Benjamin Franklin's kite experiment demonstrating the electrical nature of lightning.

As membership of Masonic lodges grew after 1717, Freemasonry became attractive to other Fellows of the Royal Society. Many were closely involved in promoting new lodges and developing the constitutional basis of the new Grand Lodge. Early lodges were sometimes a forum for lectures on scientific subjects. John Theophilus Desaguliers was both an important publicist for Newton's scientific ideas and a leading Freemason.

By the end of the 1700s, particularly during the long Presidency of Sir Joseph Banks, himself a Freemason, membership of the Royal Society had become a mix of working scientists and wealthy amateurs who were potential patrons and could help finance scientific research at a time before the government considered doing so itself. Many of these patrons were also Freemasons and thus met with scientists at the Royal Society and in lodge.

As the professionalisation of science developed in the nineteenth century, Fellows began to be elected solely on the merit of their scientific work. New types of science developed, and science education expanded with the growth of university science degrees and medical schools. Freemasonry attracted these scientist Fellows in the growing number of new lodges whose membership was drawn from particular universities, hospitals or other specialist groups.

Is Freemasonry a science?

If science is a systematically organised body of knowledge on a particular subject, then Freemasonry is indeed a science. Writes Masonic author Albert Mackey:

> *Freemasons are now expected to be more learned than formerly in all that relates to the 'science' of the Order. Its origin, its history, its objects, are now considered worthy of the attentive consideration of its disciples. The rational explanation of its ceremonies and symbols, and their connection with ancient systems of religion and philosophy, are now considered as necessary topics of inquiry for all who desire to distinguish themselves as proficient in Masonic science.*

Science is the study of the laws and substances of nature, and philosophy is careful thought about the fundamental nature of the world, the grounds for human knowledge, and the evaluation of human conduct. Both involve the pursuit of truth. This is the very basis of Masonic teaching, thus qualifying Freemasonry as a science.

Masonic science is progressive in that the initiate progresses through a series of degrees in his gradual, systematic education. The extent of the initiate's learning depends on the assiduity with which he applies himself to the work.

The Masonic degrees are designed for the gradual advancement of knowledge. With the information from each degree in hand, one chooses to limit or extend his inquiries to attain a greater or lesser amount of information, as one would in pursuing university degrees. Receiving the Masonic degrees without further study into their meaning is the equivalent of an Associate's degree; delving deeper into the mysteries and their metaphysical, neurological and philosophical lessons is akin to pursuing a Doctoral degree. How far you wish to take your studies is up to you.

Science is both a body of knowledge and a process. Freemasonry may be said to encompass many sciences. It is all of the following; the sum of which parts comprises the total *Science of Freemasonry*:

- The Science of Symbolism
- The Science of Allegory
- Moral Science
- The Science of Initiation
- The Science of Heightening Human Consciousness
- The Science of Regeneration of the Spirit
- Neuroscience

Just as the chemist practising the Science of Chemistry must learn the many sciences required before developing a new drug, so must the Freemason, practising the Science of Freemasonry, learn the many sciences required to transform himself from a rough ashlar to a perfect ashlar.

The Masonic method of becoming a better man is progressive and scientific, never random or superstitious.

The science of education

In the previous chapter I discussed how Masonic ritual writers were geniuses well ahead of their time. The Masonic symbol of a winding staircase adds further proof.

As a Freemason advances his knowledge through the degrees, he proceeds up a (symbolic) winding staircase from the ground floor of (symbolic) King Solomon's Temple to the middle chamber.

It is important to note that the staircase is specifically one which winds; the staircase symbolises the progression of the individual's education in life, which takes a spiral shape.

Masonic ritual writers centuries ago knew of the importance of spiral education. It wasn't until 1960, however, that the idea of spiral curriculum entered the mainstream through Jerome Bruner's book, *The Process of Education*. Bruner, a psychologist who made significant contributions to human cognitive psychology and cognitive learning theory in educational psychology[8], discussed the approach that any subject can be taught to a child if it is broken into strands or ideas that are repeatedly taught to the child with an increasing degree of complexity year after year.

The winding staircase teaches that progressive education is spiral, especially from physical/material (body) to mental (mind). To reach the top of the winding stairs and enter the symbolic middle chamber requires a spiralling process we must all undertake. Short cuts (straight lines) cannot be made lest we come up short ourselves. A car travelling up a mountain proceeds in a winding fashion, not in a straight line.

The spiral is a symbol of constant change and elevation. There is nothing stagnant about a spiral, as there should be no stagnancy in your personal advancement. It's human nature to rest on your laurels and take the easiest path (straight line). The spirality of the winding staircase reminds us not to be sucked into the comfort of stagnation. We must accept change, embrace it and move forward.

As Freemason Winston Churchill said: 'To improve is to change. To be perfect is to change often.'

One who moves along a straight line never changes direction. Author C.S. Lewis was correct when he said:

It may be hard for an egg to turn into a bird: it would be a jolly sight harder for it to learn to fly while remaining an egg. We are like eggs at present. And you cannot go on indefinitely being just an ordinary, decent egg. We must be hatched or go bad.

Masonic author Albert Mackey, writes of ascension to the middle chamber:

It is here that the intellectual education of the candidate begins...where childhood ends and manhood begins, he finds stretching out before him a winding stair which invites him, as it were, to ascend, and which as the symbol of discipline and instruction, teaches him that here must commence Masonic labour – here he must enter upon those glorious though difficult researches, the end of which is to be the possession of divine truth... He cannot stand still if he would be worthy of his vocation; his destiny as an immortal being requires him to ascend, step by step, until the summit, where the treasures of knowledge await him.[9]

If all nature is spiral, and man is a part of nature, then man's educational process must also be spiral. Just as nature grows spirally, so do we humans grow intellectually and spiritually via a spiral system. We are a part of nature and therefore part of the spiralling process. This is the lesson of the Masonic winding staircase. To ascend in a spiral is not the shortest route to the top but is the only route by which we truly advance. There may be a straight-line shortcut, but such a route is just that – an incomplete shortcut.

Freemasonry is a science, of that there is no doubt. The symbol of the winding staircase is a lesson on education via spiral curriculum, proving once again that the Masonic ritual writers were geniuses well ahead of their time. Yet only through the committed study of Masonic symbolism – the assiduity with which one applies himself to the work – are the deeper lessons of the Craft attained.

Remember: *It is the glory of God to conceal a thing, but it's the glory of a king to discover it*

— 4 —
All about allegory

Freemasonry is 'veiled in allegory'. Having already established what allegory is, we will now examine how allegory works as an effective means of communicating metaphysical, neurological, moral and philosophical lessons.

Remembering that *It is the glory of God to conceal a thing, but it's the glory of a king to discover it to discover it*, removing the veil of allegory relies on the assiduity of the individual in his advancement through the progressive science of Freemasonry.

Put simply, Freemasonry provides the ingredients – it is your responsibility to discover the recipe.

No spoon feeding

Freemasonry does not offer its lessons on a silver platter. Initiates are provided with working tools, allegories and other symbols to spark learning. How brightly the fire burns is up to the individual.

In the Entered Apprentice degree, we're handed the common gavel and taught to use it for the divesting our hearts and consciences of all the vices and superfluities of life.

Surely that's not the only lesson taught by the common gavel, right?

Of course not! It is your responsibility through contemplation, meditation, and research to discover the deeper lessons behind the working tools.

Masonic ritual provides only one sentence on how to employ the common gavel in your daily life. In my book *Know Thyself: Using the Symbols of Freemasonry to Improve your Life,* you'll find an entire 2,500-word chapter dedicated to the common gavel.

The Bible as a scientific handbook

Freemasonry exhorts its initiates to study the Volume of the Sacred Law, not for religious purposes, but because the Bible contains scientific teachings veiled in allegory. It is, we are told, *the greatest Light in Masonry*

– that Light which has for centuries been the rule and guide of Freemasons.

The Bible is a metaphysical handbook. One does not have to be religious to appreciate the extraordinary lessons contained within the Bible about who we are, where we came from, and how to achieve our ultimate self.

As with the teachings of Freemasonry, these lessons are concealed in allegory. Those who take Bible stories on face value and accept them as actual events involving actual people existing in actual places in a specific time period on Earth, completely miss the metaphysical lessons the Bible writers concealed beneath the surface.

Likewise, Freemasons who believe the death of Hiram Abiff at the hands of three ruffians was an actual event involving actual people existing in actual places in a specific time period, fail to uncover the concealed 'secrets' of the Craft.

To further explain the use of allegory, let's take a familiar Bible 'story' and plumb its depths for the concealed meaning.

We'll start at the very beginning with Genesis 1:1. On face value it's the story of an all-powerful God creating heaven, earth, the seas, the animals and man. But as you will see, the Bible begins with a scientific explanation of who we are and where we came from.

Interpretation of a Biblical Allegory

In the beginning God created the heaven and the earth.

Don't think of God as some Gandalf-like wizard with magical powers sitting on a throne in the sky. Think of God as consciousness – Supreme Consciousness – that exists outside of our reality. Supreme Consciousness is free of the restrictions of time and space.

Supreme Consciousness creates 'heaven', which is not some magical place where angels strum harps amidst golden clouds. Heaven is the higher consciousness of the human mind.

Earth is symbolic of matter, which is man, the vehicle into which consciousness will be placed, which is Supreme Consciousness's end goal.

And the earth was without form, and void; and darkness was upon the face of the deep.

Man (earth) is the vehicle for the previously created consciousness (heaven). But consciousness is not yet within man. He is void of consciousness. He is the potential for the consciousness of God to become form, which is what Supreme Consciousness is working towards.

And the Spirit of God moved upon the face of the waters.
The waters represent the invisible, mental aspect of reality. Symbolically water has always represented consciousness. So here we see Supreme Consciousness in the process of developing what will become human consciousness placed in human matter.

And God said, let there be light: and there was light.
The only action Supreme Consciousness is capable of is thought. So here Supreme Consciousness' thought (*let there be Light*) gives spark to human consciousness. Light, then, is the creation of human consciousness, which will later be attached to physical man.

And God saw the light, that it was good: and God divided the light from the darkness.
Here Supreme Consciousness, the Universal Mind – God – is not separating physical light from physical darkness. He is separating consciousness from non-consciousness. All this is preparation for God's ultimate plan: to place consciousness into matter.

And God called the light Day, and the darkness He called Night. And the evening and the morning were the first day.
The 'Sun' has not yet been invented, so we know that this is not a literal 'day' and 'night' because you can't have one or the other without the Sun!

Day represents conscious awareness. The night is non-consciousness. Day and night represent polarity.

And God said, let there be a firmament in the midst of the waters, and let it divide the waters from the waters. And God made the firmament and divided the waters which were under the firmament from the waters which were above the firmament: and it was so.
The firmament is the mind. The mind separates the waters (higher consciousness) from the waters (lower consciousness). To move from lower consciousness to higher consciousness is a process involving the mind. The mind separates the lower self (animal, brute nature) from the higher self (the divine part of our makeup).

This act of dividing the waters (dividing consciousness) is the act of individualising the self.

And God called the firmament Heaven. And evening and the morning were the second day.
The mind is divided between the lower mind and the higher mind, the lower consciousness and the higher consciousness.

And God said, let the waters under the heaven be gathered together unto one place, and let the dry land appear: and it was so.
Here God (Supreme Consciousness, Creator, Universal Mind) finally joins the mind (heaven, human consciousness) with the body, represented by dry land. Without consciousness, our body (flesh and bone) is just dry (useless) land. When we die a physical death, consciousness leaves the body. We become dry land.

And God called the dry land Earth; and the gathering together of the waters He called the Seas: and God saw that it was good.
Earth is human matter, the physical body. The waters, or Seas, are consciousness. Seas represent all our thoughts and ideas, that contain all potentialities, i.e. sea of thoughts.

Thus God, Supreme Consciousness, the Universal Mind, the Creator, completes its mission: creating human consciousness from Supreme Consciousness and placing that consciousness in human matter.

The opening of the Bible tells us exactly who we are: a divine spark of Supreme Consciousness in physical form.

You can choose to take the opening of Genesis at face value as an event that happened at some period in history, or you can embrace it as a scientific lesson on the creation of human consciousness and conscious awareness, and the generation of the individualised mind.

Likewise, you can take Masonic allegories on face value as actual, historic events that happened, or as deeper lessons about your mind, body and spirit. But we are clearly told that Masonry is veiled in allegory, just as the Bible clearly tells us that God communicates in parables and allegories. Jesus only spoke to his followers in parables, as we're told in Matthew 13:34: 'All these things spoke Jesus unto the multitudes in parables, and without a parable spake he not unto them.'

In Psalms 78:2 God tells us: 'I will open my mouth in a parable: I will utter dark sayings of old.'

Dark sayings of old represent the ancient teachings veiled in riddles and parables. They were deemed 'dark' because of their concealment from the masses. The dark sayings are meant to be uncovered through dedicated contemplation, meditation and learning.

Let's continue a study of Genesis and explore the 'dark sayings' in the story of Adam and Eve.

As the story goes, God created Adam and placed him in the Garden of Eden. Adam is symbolic of the unity of consciousness, that is consciousness and subconsciousness working as one, connected to the Source/God/Supreme Consciousness.

Adam is placed in a deep sleep, representing a fracture of unity consciousness. Whilst asleep, God removes one of Adam's ribs and creates Eve, who is symbolic of subconsciousness. With consciousness (Adam) and subconsciousness (Eve) no longer in a state of unity and harmony, the ego (represented by the serpent) begins to pull the strings of human action. The subconscious (Eve) succumbs to the temptation of the ego (serpent) and thus we have a separation from the Source/God/Supreme Consciousness.

Genesis clearly tells us that the dictation of our actions by ego is what separates us from reattachment to Supreme Consciousness. Only by killing the ego (subduing your passions) can one raise one's consciousness and reconnect with Supreme Consciousness, to which state as symbolic Adam we all once belonged. Consciousness and subconsciousness (Adam and Eve) must work in perfect harmony to resurrect the divine spark in each of us – our attachment to Supreme Consciousness.

Nothing in the Bible or in Freemasonry is handed to us with newspaper directness. If you want to know the 'secrets' or the 'dark sayings of old' it is your duty to discover them. In doing so you will become a king!

Let's examine another well-known Bible story: Samson and Delilah.

Samson possesses superhuman strength, the source of which is his unshaven hair. Delilah, the infamous harlot, tries to extract from Samson information about the source of his strength so as to betray him to the Philistines. As the Book of Judges tells us, Delilah nagged and prodded Samson every day until he could take her nagging no more. He told her his secret: 'No razor has ever been used on my head because I have been a Nazirite dedicated to God from my mother's womb. If my head were shaved, my strength would leave me, and I would become as weak as any other man.'

Delilah waits until Samson is asleep and cuts off his hair, thus stripping him of his superhuman strength. She then betrays him to the Philistines who take him prisoner, gouge out his eyes, shackle him and send him to a prison to work as a grain grinder.

Samson asks the Lord to help him regain his hair, and thus his strength, one last time. While pushing round the grinding stone every day, Samson's hair grows back. One night he is dragged in front of a Philistine banquet to be mocked and ridiculed and asks his guide to place him between the two pillars of the temple.

While shackled between the two pillars, we are told:

Then Samson prayed to the Lord, "Sovereign Lord, remember me. Please, God, strengthen me just once more, and with one blow let me get revenge on the Philistines for gouging out my two eyes," Samson cried, "Let me die with the Philistines." Then he pushed with all his might, and down came the temple on the rulers and the people. Thus, he killed many more when he died than when he lived!

What does the story of Samson and Delilah allegorically teach us?

First, let's look at the source of Samson's strength – his hair. Samson was a man of God, with devout belief in Supreme Consciousness. This is his true super strength. Samson's long hair is the source of his spiritual strength growing forth from his mind. This strength source had been growing since he was in the womb, and had never, ever been cut off. The might of Samson's spiritual side/right brain symbolic/higher consciousness was enormous.

Delilah represents the emotions that we let take over our lives. These emotions seek to control us and drain our spiritual strength. By telling Delilah the secret of his strength, Samson makes the mistake of giving into his emotions. Now his emotions have control over him, and thus cut him off from his higher consciousness, represented by the cutting of his hair. Samson is now ruled by emotions as opposed to being ruled by spirit.

Delilah (emotions) then betrays Samson to the Philistines, who are representative of lower thought process/animal nature/brute nature/ego. The ego blinds and imprisons Samson, and makes him turn a grinding wheel day in, day out, which is representative of our lives when ruled by the ego – round and round we go, the same pattern of low vibration. However, Samson does not give up on his spiritual side, and slowly but surely his hair begins to grow back, representing his slow, difficult but necessary rise above his lower nature/ego/crude nature.

During the banquet in the temple, with the temple representing our brain, Samson asks his guide to shackle him to the two pillars, representing the pillars of duality, of higher consciousness and lower consciousness, of spirit and ego. With all the Philistines present, that is all the bad thoughts and ego of the individual, Samson tears down the two pillars killing everyone, including himself. Samson's selfless act, in which he kills himself and his Philistine captors, represents the slaying of the ego, negative thoughts and controlling emotions. This is a process which must take place in our brain for us to attain higher consciousness and reconnect with Supreme Consciousness. We must kill our ego, slay our emotions, and overcome our lower nature.

The Bible stories are all about the brain, the mind, and consciousness. This is why Jesus was crucified at Golgotha, which means 'Place of the Skull'. The brain is in the skull. Everything takes place inside the brain, inside your mind. God is consciousness – Supreme Consciousness. Supreme Consciousness is within you, which is why the Psalm writer tells us to 'Be still and know that I am God,' or in other words, through silence, meditation and introspection, you will connect with your higher consciousness, which in turn will connect with Supreme Consciousness.

The brain acts as a conduit for conscious energy; for connecting with Supreme Consciousness. The scriptures guide us to right side brain entry through meditation, which is also where Freemasonry aims to guide us through its rituals and ceremonies.

The biggest secret in Freemasonry
Like the Bible, Masonic ritual has a deeper meaning than the words on paper. This deeper meaning is about you; more specifically, it is about the inner you. Freemasonry is interior work, as it is the internal not the external qualifications of a man that Freemasonry regards. Every story, every working tool, and every symbol teaches a lesson about internal self-improvement, particularly the elevation of consciousness, from your lower to higher consciousness, which allows you to connect (reconnect) with Supreme Consciousness.

Once you make this realisation, Freemasonry becomes a marvellous tool for personal discovery and more than what you may have been taught, sitting in lodge wondering, 'What is this all about?' and 'What's the point of it all?'.

Sadly, many men give up on Freemasonry because they have not been taught how to pull back the veil. The true secrets are not communicated directly, and the experience of sitting in lodge watching circumambulations, hearing knocks, and reciting archaic words becomes a pointless exercise from which they go home without any reward but for a free meal and a glass of Scotch.

This uneducated, lazy approach to Freemasonry undertaken by many lodges swims the Craft directly into the shark's mouth. Most lodges are so intent on initiating new candidates that they neglect – or simply don't know – how to interpret the ritual and communicate its concealed teachings. Just because you repeated some words, had a blindfold removed and strapped a piece of lambskin around your waist does not make you a Mason. True Freemasonry is not that easy. It requires some actual work and dedication on your part before you will ever realise what the ritual calls 'Light' – which is all you ever asked for in your initiation. Foolish it is, don't you think, to not understand that for which you asked?

Everything in Freemasonry – every step, every sign, every working tool, every symbol and every word – has a rich symbolic meaning designed to help us understand our spiritual/internal life, and contribute towards achieving a shift in consciousness, a connection to our higher self. The knowledge is there, waiting, for those who have the gusto to unearth it. Knowledge is never given to the profane and ignorant, but only to the true seeker.

The biggest secret about Freemasonry is that it's about the brain, the mind, the thoughts that arise out of one's consciousness, and the spirit. The ritual is a lesson in psychology, metaphysics and neurology cloaked in symbols and allegories.

There are Freemasons who will shake their heads at what I've written here. For them Freemasonry is no more than reciting the ritual by heart, a bunch of lessons about morality, and the camaraderie of eating and drinking together at the festive board. They choose to swim in the shallow water.

As Nietzsche said: 'And those who were seen dancing were thought to be insane by those who could not hear the music'.

No small parts
The allegories of Freemasonry present the initiate with a story rich in metaphysical, philosophical, moral and neurological lessons.

Such lessons aren't immediately obvious, even upon witnessing the allegory in dramatic form, as during the Master Mason degree. It is the initiate's responsibility to search out the true meaning of the third degree legend.

The initiate may consider some symbols and characters to have little or no meaning at all. He may consider them simply in place to 'fill' an interesting story. Let me assure you, however, nothing in Masonic ritual exists for 'fill' – particularly not in the legend of the third degree.

The rubbish of the temple, the sprig of acacia, the seafaring man, the wayfaring man, and the brow of a hill may seem insignificant elements of the Hiramic legend, but the genius ritual writers concealed important metaphysical and neurological lessons in each.

For example, why does the seafaring man refuse to grant the three ruffians passage to Ethiopia in the following brief exchange from the third degree?

Ruffian No 3: Yonder is a sea-faring man. Let us accost him.
Ruffian No 3: Is that your ship there?
S-F: It is.
Ruffian No 3: Where are you bound?
S-F: To Ethiopia.
Ruffian No 3: When do you sail?
S-F: Immediately.
Ruffian No 3: Do you take passengers?
S-F: I do.
Ruffian No 3: Will you take us?
S-F: I will if you have King Solomon's permit to leave the country.
Ruffian No 3: We will pay your demands, but we have no permits.
S-F: Then you cannot go, for I am strictly forbidden to take any of the workmen from the Temple out of the country without King Solomon's permit.
Ruffian No 3: Then let us return back into the country.

In ancient art, water symbolised consciousness. To cross water is to cross from a state of lower consciousness to higher consciousness.
- Moses parts the Red Sea (water) leading the Hebrews from lower consciousness (Egypt under the reign of Pharaoh) to higher consciousness.
- Christ (higher consciousness) walks on water. When he asks Peter to walk on water, at first Peter is fine. But as soon as Peter begins to fear earthly things such as the wind, the mind of his lower nature takes over and he's convinced he will drown. Peter is not yet able to rid himself of his ego, and therefore cannot cross the water to a state of higher consciousness.

- In the movie *Life of Pi*, Pi Patel spends almost the entire film on a boat in the water. He must learn to overcome his ego – his fears – and embrace faith in God and positive thinking that eventually leads him to a happier state of existence, allegorically representative of an ascendance in consciousness. To reach a state of higher consciousness, we endure ordeals that test our faith and character.
- In the movie *Groundhog Day,* Phil Connors begins to actively change the monotony of his days (his lower consciousness) by stepping over the street puddle (water). He thus begins his symbolic journey to a state of higher consciousness, which he achieves by ridding himself of his rampant ego through performance of selfless deeds for the betterment of others.
- At the end of the film *Being There*, Chance Gardner walks on water. He is able to do this because he is wholly unaware of his limitations. The ego is what places limitations on our capabilities. Without the shackles of the ego and having acted selflessly towards others with kindness and goodness in his every expression, Chance has symbolically overcome his animal nature. Pure and void of base thoughts, Chance is elevated to a higher state of being than the rest of us, hence his ability to walk on water (as did Christ).

The seafaring man in the Masonic third degree acts as a gatekeeper of sorts to our higher consciousness. He refuses passage to the three ruffians because they have not yet learned the life lessons needed to transcend their lower nature.

To travel on water represents the attainment of a state of mind above our animal self. The murderous ruffians are driven by ego, lusts and desires. Their inability to crush their ego and transcend their animal nature flat out denies them the right to travel on the waters of higher consciousness.

The ruffians, by their own words, choose to 'accost' the seafaring man, not to approach him with kindness. One cannot pay for, demand or force oneself into a state of higher consciousness.

The ship or boat symbolises the desire to transcend existence, that is, the desire to move above and beyond the shackles of the earthly ego. For a greater examination of boat symbolism, let's look at the most famous boat in the Bible, Noah's Ark.

Noah was a 'just' man who lived a spiritual life instead of an ego-driven existence. The rest of the world weren't so spiritually inclined. God decided He'd had enough of their wickedness, specifically their terrible thoughts, and sent a great flood to cleanse the planet. (Remember, this is an allegory and not an actual event that took place at some specific moment in history)

Noah survived the flood upon an ark he built. This is important to note: God did not build the ark for Noah, as God does not simply hand us access to our higher consciousness. He provides the tools and materials, but we have to do the work ourselves.

Transcendent as he was of his lower nature, Noah lived a life of higher consciousness. As such he was able to rise above the earth (lower thoughts) in his ark and survive the flood.

Representing the mind at rest, free from the clutches of the ego, Noah brings salvation to both himself and his family.

The three ruffians seek the same sort of salvation.

Why specifically is the seafaring man set to travel to Ethiopia and not some other destination?

Said to be the location of the Garden of Eden, Ethiopia represents a higher plane of being.

So here we have the lower mind (our ego driven nature – the three ruffians) attempting to gain access to a higher state of consciousness without partaking in the necessary processes required to achieve such ascension.

The seafaring man refuses passage because selfishness, lust, and ignorance have no place in higher consciousness. If one possesses any of these lower mind characteristics, he will be denied passage to a plane of higher consciousness.

You'd better believe that if Noah possessed any lust, ignorance or selfishness, he would have been wiped out by God's flood instead of being set adrift to safety.

This small section of the third degree shows, once again, how Freemasonry is a user's manual describing the proper function and potential of the human being. The end goal is the realisation of a state of being greater than we presently exhibit, but which we presently contain.

Like the three ruffians, we are stuck in the lower realms of creation and are struggling to transcend our mental, ego-driven body ruled by degenerate thinking, feeling and actions. If we do not clean up and polish our mental, emotional and physical bodies, we will be denied passage to (symbolic) Ethiopia.

We must master ourselves. This is the sublime philosophy and universal science once taught in the great mystery schools of antiquity and currently promoted in the superstructure of Freemasonry.

– 5 –
A science of symbols

The Science of Freemasonry encompasses many sciences, one of which is the Science of Symbolism.

Freemasonry is the Science of Symbolism, yet symbolism is not unique to Freemasonry. Every day, often without realising it, we use symbols to decipher information.

Symbols are an inevitable part of life. They are all around us. The purpose of a symbol is to transmit information to your brain in a direct way without the use of words. Symbols convey an abstract idea that would require sentences or even paragraphs of text to relate.

- We know which bathroom to enter in a public place by seeing the symbol of a man, a woman or a handicap sign.
- A series of curved lines increasing in size tells us the strength of the WiFi connection on our computer.
- A zig-zag line on our phone is a symbol of the battery charging.
- The colours on traffic lights are symbols of what action to take when driving.
- When the symbol of a seatbelt lights up on an airplane, we know it's time to clip in.
- An arrow is a symbol telling us which direction to take.

Those golden arches
Corporations use symbols as a means for customers to identify their products.

We are all familiar with the McDonalds golden arches, BMW's white propeller spinning in a blue sky, Nike's swoosh, the triple stripe of Adidas, the bitten apple on our iPhone or iPad, and the Macy's star.

Symbols allow businesses to communicate their brand without words. For example, did you know the Adidas triple stripe is actually a mountain range? It symbolises the challenges of life we must all overcome, for which a pair of reliable Adidas shoes is helpful.[10]

Book lovers will be well aware of the symbol used by online retailer Amazon, which features a curved line under the company name. The line begins under the letter 'A' and finishes under the letter 'Z'. In essence, the symbol is a smile because that is what happens when you realise you can buy everything on Amazon, from A to Z!

A symbol is an object that represents, stands for or suggests an idea, visual image, belief, action, or material entity. Various faiths use symbols to represent their doctrines. When we see a cross, the words 'church' or 'Christian Church' are not necessary – the symbol conveys the message. A synagogue does not need the words 'Jewish Temple' or 'Jewish Synagogue' posted above its entrance – the Star of David serves this purpose symbolically without the use of words.

The soul of Masonry

The symbols of Freemasonry convey material, moral, spiritual and metaphysical lessons on how a person should live their life, and the harmonious operation of the body, mind and spirit. To truly understand Freemasonry, one must understand its symbols. It is impossible to understand the enormous scope of Masonic thought and teaching without interpretation of its symbols.[11]

Albert Pike wrote: 'The symbolism of Masonry is, in my opinion, the soul of Masonry.'

Common Masonic symbols such as the square and compasses, the plumb line, the common gavel, the 24-inch gauge, the trowel, the beehive, the Ionic, Doric and Corinthian pillars, and the sprig of acacia convey messages to the conscious and subconscious without the need for words.

Writes Daniel Beresniak in *Symbols of Freemasonry:* 'Symbolism looks at the world as if it were a text. It involves thinking about thought and speaking about language. As its etymology suggests, a symbol is an image made up of various elements in such a way that the whole represents more than the sum of its parts.'

Beresniak points out that the first degree initiation ritual states: 'Here all is symbol.' The initiate is taught to look at the symbolic nature of everything that exists.

'In other words,' writes Beresniak, 'everything should be seen as a metaphor. This point must be stressed because symbolism is so often looked upon as merely a codified language, recognisable to members of the same group and nothing more.'[12]

A slow process

There is no fast-track to learning and internalising Masonic symbolism. Uncovering a symbolic system is like imbibing fine Scotch whisky; you need to nose it, drink it, add a few drops of water, nose it again, drink it some more, swirl it around, understand the peatiness, the fruitiness, the cask influences of sherry or bourbon, and then experience the finish. Like a dram of Lagavulin 16 or Ardbeg 10, Masonic symbolism is a drink to be savoured, studied, enjoyed and internalised, never to be tossed 'down the hatch.'

The genius authors of Masonic ritual and symbolism knew that symbols are an effective means of communication because the subconscious mind thinks in symbols. They carried on a tradition that the mystery schools taught in Ancient Greece, Egypt, Babylon, Rome and Sumeria. Symbols are geometrical and mathematical constructs which then resonate with the interior of the brain, which also decodes things mathematically and geometrically. The subconscious mind thinks in the form of images. All your experiences and memories are stored in the subconscious mind. How are they stored? In the form of symbols and images, which is why when we dream all we see are symbols and pictures, dreams being the thoughts of the subconscious mind.

In his amazing essay entitled 'An Introduction to the Principles of Masonic Ritual' on the website virtual-loi.co.uk, author Lucius Dell'Alba explains how Masonic ritual imprints symbolic lessons on the mind:

> *Because the primary function of the mind is pattern recognition and to look for meaning in those patterns, when an experience occurs the first thing that happens is a search for similar experiences.*
>
> *Recognition occurs because many of the same neurons are fired and this is detected by consciousness.*
>
> *If a similar experience is found in memory, then a conclusion is drawn as to the meaning of that experience based upon the cumulative similar experiences from the past. This means that any particular type of experience comes to symbolise a particular meaning. This is the start of what becomes a symbolic language and this is how the subconscious thinks. If you can present the subconscious with an experience (such as a particular image together with a particular sound or word) and you can instil that event with a specific meaning, then the subconscious will pick that up. It has effectively*

learned a new symbolic 'word' for its vocabulary of meaningful experiences. This is how the subconscious works naturally and it is these functions that ritual work employs to teach the hidden mysteries in Freemasonry. So, the key to talking to the subconscious is the use of symbols.[13]

Dell'Alba goes on to explain the link between experience and symbol:

It is also possible to present symbols to the subconscious and induce specific meaningful experiences at the same time and therefore link the symbol to that experience. Whenever the individual encounters that symbol from thereon, there will be a tendency to recall the emotion or experience that was induced when it was presented. This is the key to all ritual work.'

Allegories are symbols too

Words also have symbolic import. An allegory is verbal symbolism, writes Albert G Mackey in *The Symbolism of Freemasonry: Illustrating and Explaining Its Science and Philosophy Its Legends, Myths and Symbols*:

Allegory itself is nothing else but verbal symbolism; it is the symbol of an idea, or of a series of ideas, not presented to the mind in an objective and visible form, but clothed in language, and exhibited in the form of a narrative. And therefore ... Freemasonry is a science of morality, developed and inculcated by the ancient method of symbolism, which gives its whole identity to Freemasonry, and has caused it to differ from every other association that the ingenuity of man has devised. It is this that has bestowed upon it that attractive form which has always secured the attachment of its disciples and its own perpetuity.

Mackey further writes: 'Withdraw from Freemasonry its symbolism, and you take from the body its soul, leaving behind nothing but a lifeless mass of effete matter, fitted only for a rapid decay.'

You power the symbol

A symbol is only empowered by your interpretation, just as a car is only powered by gas. Without gas, a car is just a shell. Without interpretation, a symbol is just a drawing. A symbol carries as much or as little power as you *choose* to invest it with.

Everything in life is a choice. If you choose to let a cross, a rainbow flag, a hammer and sickle, or a crescent moon have power over you, it will. If you choose not to let these symbols affect you, they remain mere drawings.

A triangle drawn with crayons by a 4-year-old in kindergarten does not radiate any great power or convey any sublime message or truth. It is, simply, a triangle. To the high school geometry student, the same triangle is symbolic of the Pythagoras Theorem, $a^2 + b^2 = c^2$. To the Freemason, a triangle is symbolic of the complete man in whom the three sides of the triangle represent the three aspects of a person: physical, mental, spiritual; or mind, body and spirit. To the Satanist, the triangle – known as a thaumaturgic triangle – is a symbol used for casting spells or summoning demons.

A symbol is only as powerful as you allow. Sometimes, in fact most of the time, a triangle is just…a triangle!

According to conspiracy theorists, all the basic shapes we learn to draw as children – triangles, squares, circles, stars – are symbols of Satanism or the 'illuminati'. Other innocent symbols such as the sun, the moon, water, arches, pyramids, and even dots are also considered sinister. Why? Because conspiracy theorists empower these symbols as such.

Take, for example, the symbol of retail giant, the Target Corporation. It's a circle with a dot in the middle otherwise known as – wait for it – a target! But according to some conspiracy theorists the logo represents a penis (the dot) inside a vagina (the circle) and is therefore symbolic of pagan phallic worship. To the rest of us the Target logo is simply a target.

Symbols mean to us that which we interpret them to mean. A black cat means bad luck in the USA but good luck in Japan. A cross means little more to a Buddhist than two intersecting lines but is the central symbol in the Christian belief system.

Symbolic meaning is also attached to numbers. The number seven is considered lucky by most and the number 13 symbolises bad luck. There is even a name for the fear of the number 13: triskaidekaphobia. Those who interpret '13' as a symbol of bad luck will not stay on the 13th floor of a hotel and fear any Friday that falls on the 13th day of the month. Why are they scared? Not because of any proven fact that '13' brings bad luck but because they choose to empower the number as a symbol of misfortune.

Progressive science, progressive symbol

Freemasonry is regarded as a progressive science, and the square and compasses is a progressive symbol that changes appearance according to degree.

In the first degree of Freemasonry (Entered Apprentice) the two legs of the compasses sit below the two legs of the square.

In the second degree (Fellowcraft) one leg of the compasses sits above the square and the other remains below the square.

Freemasonry's Progressive Science is represented in the position of the square and compass through the three degrees

In the third degree (Master Mason) both legs of the compasses sit above the square, and it is this representation that is most commonly seen outside of a Masonic lodge.

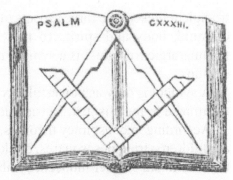

The progression of the symbols continues when a Mason becomes a Past Master – having served a term as an elected and installed Master of a lodge – and the square is replaced by a quadrant, or one-fourth of a circle.

The Masonic square is an angle of ninety degrees and by it a Mason is taught to square his actions. In the symbolism of the square and compasses, however, the square represents man's base self, that is, your animal nature. This is the part of you which, simply speaking, is your lowest self.

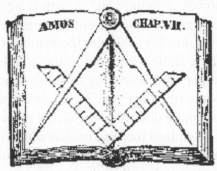

Also known as 'brute nature' or 'material nature' your lowest self is the crudest version of you; the part of your make up that is unrefined, rough, primitive and unaltered by any processing. The lowest self centres on the ego, which is made up of such components as: pride,

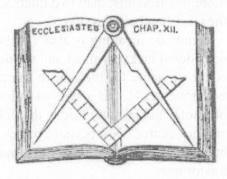

guilt, aggression, anger, hate, selfishness, skepticism, conditional love, hostility, jealousy, lust, addictions, elitism, illusion, denial, conformity, boredom, the need for attention and validation, and the lack of realisation of the divinity in oneself.

The square is, in essence, the unrefined man. But how does it represent such? Squares are not found in visible nature. There are no square trees, no square clouds, no square animals, no square body parts and no square rocks. Therefore, a square is something man made, hence the square in the Masonic square and compasses represents man.

The Masonic compasses are always opened to 60° (one-third of 180° of an equilateral triangle, representing man balanced in mind, body and spirit). Emblematically the compasses teach a Mason to circumscribe his desires and keep his passions in due bounds with all mankind.

In the symbolism of the square and compasses, however, the compasses represent your higher self (the one-third of the 180° that represents spirit), your spiritual aspects, which are capable of higher thoughts – of a life beyond the material, physical base nature.

Compasses draw circles, and circles are found in visible nature. Therefore, the compasses represent God, the Creator, a Higher Power. As such they represent man's inner divinity, the divine spark, the higher self. Placing the compasses atop the square represents the entire purpose of Freemasonry: to improve oneself and progress above one's base nature. By doing so, a Freemason endeavours to become the best human being he can, transcending his ego and embracing his higher self, the part of him that is God-like.

The progression explained

As an Entered Apprentice, the newly made Mason has not yet learned how to rise above his base nature, therefore the points of the compasses (higher self) are below the square, as his base nature (square) still dominates his thoughts and actions.

As a Fellowcraft (second degree), he is on his way to transcending his base nature and so one point of the compasses sits above the square.

As a Master Mason (third degree) a Mason is said to have learned the lessons necessary to transcend his base nature, check his ego at the door, and embrace his higher self. Both points of the compasses are now positioned over the square as the higher self symbolically has control over the lower self.

What is transcendence?

Transcendence is true freedom and what separates us from animals. It is our remarkable human capacity to climb above programmed responses to outer variables and discover causality inside.

Transcendence is the freed awareness which has arrived at such level of improvement that it can see itself as the reason and is no longer a slave to the conditioning of society and environment.

Transcendence will reveal your real self. Not the self characterised by associations with your outer self (how you look, your job, your marriage, your hobbies, your lusts, your material desires) but the self characterised by the completely cognisant standard vitalising the psychophysical framework. It is the union between the awareness and the vitality, the dynamic rule that enlivens you, and not simply one of several adapted responses to the external influences in your life.

Most people characterise themselves in connection to their external selves. This is human nature. We perceive ourselves to be what we see in the mirror. We characterise ourselves by our sensitivity to our exterior. Our actual extraordinary nature is the cognisance of ourselves as totally free from such outer definitions.

Only through symbols

I will give the last word on symbols here to prolific Masonic author, Albert Mackey, who wrote:

> *Of the various modes of communicating instruction to the uninformed, the masonic student is particularly interested in two; namely, the instruction by legends and that by symbols. It is to these two, almost exclusively, that he is indebted for all that he knows, and for all that he can know, of the philosophic system which is taught in the institution. All its mysteries and its dogmas, which constitute its philosophy, are intrusted for communication to the neophyte, sometimes to one, sometimes to the other of these two methods of instruction, and sometimes to both of them combined. The Freemason has no way of reaching any of these esoteric teachings of the Order except through the media of a legend or symbol.[14]*

– 6 –
Never, never, never die

'Divine spark' is a term you will come across many times in this book. What is your divine spark and why is it important?

Chemistry tells us that 96 percent of the human body is made up of just four elements:[15]

oxygen - 65%
carbon - 18%
hydrogen - 9.5%
nitrogen - 3.2%

Most of these are contained in water.

The other 4 percent comprises approximately 60 chemical elements including copper, iodine, selenium, manganese, cobalt and molybdenum, which is important for transforming sulphur into a usable form.

We know the exact chemical components of the body, but if you put oxygen, carbon, hydrogen, nitrogen and the other elements in a test tube, you would not be able to make a human being due to the lack of one key ingredient: consciousness.

What is consciousness?

What is consciousness? is a question debated since time immemorial.

According to the *Merriam-Webster* dictionary, consciousness is the state or quality of awareness, or, of being aware of an external object or something within oneself. It has been defined variously as awareness, the ability to experience or to feel, wakefulness, having a sense of selfhood or soul. Consciousness has also been described as the executive control system of the mind.[16]

Consciousness cannot be studied under a microscope and cannot be replicated by human hands.

Consciousness comes from a source greater than the physical world, a source known by many names depending on one's interpretation and/or belief system:

- God
- The Centre
- Supreme Consciousness
- The Universal Mind

The Grand Architect of the Universe

Freemasonry uses the term 'Grand Architect of the Universe' to describe the source of consciousness.

Anti-Masons claim that the Grand Architect is a false-god worshipped by Freemasons. This is, of course, ridiculous. There is no Masonic god, but Freemasons do profess belief in a Supreme Being. While this Supreme Being may go by any number of names – God, Allah, Jehovah, Brahma – it is not the specific being that is important but rather what the Supreme Being represents, which is Supreme Consciousness (Absolute Consciousness, Universe Consciousness), the non-physical source of human consciousness.

From Supreme Consciousness we receive our earthly animation and states of lower and higher consciousness. Through consciousness we are the architects of our own existence, shaping our lives by our thoughts and actions.

Supreme Consciousness is the Grand Architect that gives us the ability to think, feel and act. An architect is one who plans, designs and reviews the construction of buildings. The Grand Architect is one who plans, designs and reviews the construction of all life, and all things visible and invisible. The Grand Architect is Supreme Consciousness. Just as an architect is inside the home you live in, as his consciousness bore the designs and plans that constructed the abode, so too is the Grand Architect (Supreme Consciousness) inside you. This connection to Supreme Consciousness which resides inside you is your divine spark.

Indian philosopher and yogi, Shrii Shrii Anandamurti, says:

> *The Supreme Consciousness is there in you as the oil is in the oilseed. Crush the seed through spiritual practice (sádhaná) and you attain Him; separate the mind from Consciousness and you will see that the resplendence of the Supreme Consciousness illuminates your whole inner being. He is there like butter in curd; churn it and He will appear from within. Churn your mind through spiritual practice and God will appear like butter from curd. He is like a subterranean river*

*in you. Remove the sands of mind and you will find the clear,
cool waters within.*[17]

An inextinguishable flame

Connection to Supreme Consciousness exists as an inextinguishable flame
inside each of us. This is the part of us that is perfect, unblemished and
pure, and a divine extension of the Source/the Centre/God.

Masonic ritual makes mention of the divine spark in no uncertain terms.
The third degree lecture tells us of an 'imperishable part within us' that is
our direct connection to Supreme Consciousness and will never die. In
fact, this point is of such great importance that the word 'never' is used
three times. The imperishable divine spark will 'never, never, never die.'

1 Corinthians 3:16 tells us that God/Supreme Consciousness/Absolute
Consciousness/Universal Consciousness resides inside us.

*Know ye not that you are the temple of God, and that the spirit of God
dwelleth in you.*

The writer of Luke's gospel delivers the same message: '...The
Kingdom of God cometh not with observation. Neither shall they say, Lo
here! Or lo there! For behold, the Kingdom of God is within you!'

The divine spark is the piece of Supreme Consciousness in us all. The
human brain acts as a conduit of the energy of Supreme Consciousness.
Supreme Consciousness is infinite but is limited by the ego when processed
by the brain within the human body. Only by crucifying the ego or, as
Freemasonry terms it, by the search for 'light', 'more light' and 'further
light' attained through 'subduing the passions and improving oneself in
Freemasonry' can we expand our consciousness, break free of the ego's
shackles and ignite our divine spark.

As we rise, ego must fall. The potential energy within must be raised
from the grave, just as Grand Master Hiram Abiff was symbolically raised
from a dead level to a living perpendicular.

Raising one's consciousness to a connection with Supreme
Consciousness is the ultimate aim of Freemasonry. Activating your divine
spark will allow you to reconnect to the force behind all nature and
existence, which has no self-concerns and no limitations – a pathway to a
non-physical sense far greater than the physical reality that currently holds
your divine spark in a very small, limited box waiting to be opened. Said
Indian philosopher Pandit Shriram Sharma: 'The universe is founded in
consciousness and guided by it. The final reality is Universal
Consciousness (God). This Supreme Consciousness is Omnipresent i.e.

present everywhere. Its evolutionary powers pervade the entire Universe. All processes of Nature are governed by the laws of this Absolute Force.'

The divine spark is triggered by introspection processes. It is your energetic epicentre and can help improve quality of life. Through processes of unlocking your divine spark, you will balance the energy levels in your body and be better enabled to meet your goals by having a clear image of what you wish to achieve. You will feel more motivated and positive. By having a positive energetic vibration, you will influence the positive energies around you and attract greater positivity to your life.

Think of your divine spark in terms of something anatomical, which is operative as much as it is speculative or philosophical.

More than monkey relatives

It is hard to believe that a being as amazing as a human is a mere aggregation of matter and elements that work perfectly in an established order. Our body is too complicated to be solely matter. There needs to be something that connects us with something superior and extraordinary, and that something is the divine spark, the sign that we are more than monkey relatives; more than blood, bone and elements in the periodic table. We are divine energy manifest in flesh.

The divine spark is an energetic charge we receive at the moment of conception, through the miracle of life creation. According to Gnostic beliefs, this spark is a gift from God, which we must activate during our lifetime through actions and experiences. Thus, since it is a divine fragment, it will guide us towards love, harmony, and peace, keeping in mind that love is the greatest energy in the universe. 'Love is the only reality and it is not a mere sentiment,' said playwright and essayist, Rabindranath Tagore. 'It is the ultimate truth that lies at the heart of Creation. From love the world is born, by love it is sustained, towards love it moves, and into love it enters.'

To activate your divine spark is to turn inward and connect with your centre. You must find a key to unlock your divine spark and jailbreak it from your material-centric life. Some achieve this through prayer or meditation, others through yoga, music or martial arts. For centuries, the practice of Freemasonry has proven a key to unlocking and activating the divine spark. As esteemed Masonic author Albert Pike wrote: 'Freemasonry is the subjugation of the Human that is in man by the Divine.'[18]

The aim of Freemasonry is to bring under control our material desires to enable the rise of our divine spark, that is, the part of us that is perfect, unblemished and pure, that can never be extinguished and is a divine extension of a higher power. This elevation of consciousness being the crux of Freemasonry, you understand why so many successful people throughout the centuries committed a vast amount of their time to the study of Masonic symbolism as a means of turning inward and connecting with their centre to unleash the power of their divine spark.

Masonic author Manly P. Hall wrote that: '…behind these diverse forms there is one connected Life Principle, the spark of God in all living things…this divine spark shines out as brightly from the body of a foe as it does from the dearest friend.'[19]

– 7 –

The Lion of the Tribe of Judah

Seemingly insignificant allegorical references in Masonic ritual contain metaphysical and neurological lessons, an example of which is reference to the lion of the tribe of Judah in the Master Mason degree.

Having witnessed the failed attempts to raise the body of Grand Master Hiram Abiff (GMHA) by the grip of an Entered Apprentice, and then by the grip of a Fellowcraft, King Solomon tells the Masons in attendance: '…and though the skin may slip from the flesh, and the flesh cleaves from the bones, there is strength in the lion of the tribe of Judah, and he shall prevail.'

Remembering that Freemasonry teaches via symbols and allegory, it should be clear that King Solomon is not talking about an actual lion.

Camp to the East

The second section of the third degree ritual involves the dramatisation of the death and raising of GMHA. Note, I do not say death and 'resurrection' as the word 'resurrection' implies a return to physical life after the physical death of the body, which is an impossibility.

GMHA did not experience physical resurrection. His dead body never came back to life. His lifeless body was raised from the ground (from a horizontal to a perpendicular) but he was never miraculously reanimated, as some mistakenly believe.

It is also wrong, in my opinion, for some Masonic jurisdictions to use the Ancient Landmark: 'Belief in the resurrection of the body'. Freemasonry teaches that there is life beyond the body, that is, beyond the physical vehicle. Dead bodies do not reanimate. GMHA is not Frankenstein's monster or one of *The Walking Dead*.

Getting back to the specifics of King Solomon's words at the grave of GMHA, we need to ask the question: Why does King Solomon choose the lion of the tribe of Judah as his method of raising the body of GMHA? After all, there were twelve tribes of Israel and many of their banners featured animals, including the donkey of the tribe of Issachar; the wolf of the tribe of Benjamin; the serpent of the tribe of Dan; and the gazelle of the tribe of Naphtali.

Freemasonry tells us that the Holy Bible is the 'rule and guide' for our practice, so we should necessarily turn to its pages for part of our answer.

In Numbers 2:3 we read: 'And on the East side toward the rising of the Sun shall they of the standards of the camp of Judah pitch throughout their armies.'

Of particular interest is the word 'East' and reference to the Sun. The Worshipful Master of the lodge sits in the East, as the East has always been a place of wisdom and enlightenment. The Fellowcraft lecture tells us: 'Ages ago, upon the Eastern plains, was our institution set up, founded upon principles more durable than the metal wrought into the statues of ancient kings.'

In the candidate's search for Light, he is lead in an Easterly direction, as we see in the following exchange:

WM: Whence came you and whither are you travelling?

SD (answering for candidate): From the West travelling East.

WM: Why did you leave the West and travel East?

SD (answering for the candidate): In search of Light in Masonry.

The Worshipful Master sits in the East to 'open and govern the Lodge'. He represents the Sun rising in the East to 'open and govern the day,' and it is from the East that he dispenses wisdom. The chair in which he sits is known as the Oriental Chair, the word 'Orient' meaning 'situated in or belonging to the East'.

Once again, as all in Freemasonry is taught via symbol and allegory, we must determine the symbolic import of the East?

It's all about the brain

There are two hemispheres of the brain: left and right. They look similar but perform very different functions.

Left Brain Functions:

Analytic Thought

Logic

Language

Reasoning

Science and Math

Number Skills

Written Word

Right Brain Functions:
Creativity
Art Awareness
Imagination
Intuition
Insight
Holistic Thought
Music Awareness

When King Solomon states that there is strength in the Lion of the Tribe of Judah, he is saying that the only way to raise oneself symbolically from a dead horizontal to a living perpendicular is to use the functions of the right side of the brain. This is why we camp to the East, the right brain hemisphere.

Transcendence and an elevation of one's consciousness will not come about scientifically or mathematically, which are left brain functions. Elevation of consciousness requires intuition, higher emotions, and a holistic thought process, which are all right brain functions.

In short, the right side represents our higher spiritual nature. It is this aspect of our nature that raises the master, not the logic and intellect, physicality and concreteness of the left side.

The ancient scriptures constantly admonish us to use the right-side functions of our brain, as it is there that God is said to dwell in the holy of holies of the temple:

1 Kings 6:8: 'The door for the middle chamber was in the *right* side of the house: and they went up with winding stairs into the middle chamber, and out of the middle into the third.'

Psalms 16:11: 'You will show me the path of life: in your presence is fullness of joy; at your *right* hand there are pleasures for evermore.'

Ecclesiastes 10:2: 'A wise man's heart is at his *right* hand; but a fool's heart at his left.'

Matthew 25:33: 'And he shall set the sheep on his *right* hand, but the goats on the left.'

To raise the master is to raise yourself above your lower nature and experience your divine self, understanding that divinity dwells in us all. Stimulating the right side of the brain separates us from the thoughts of the left side and elevates us above our lower nature. Only through accessing the right brain functions can one break free of the ego's grip. This is what King Solomon refers to when raising GMHA from the grave.

Let's go fishing

A memorable gospel story about right brain function appears in John 21, when Christ appeared to his disciples at the Sea of Galilee.

Simon Peter told them, 'I am going fishing'.

'We will go with you', they said. So, they went out and got into the boat, but caught nothing that night.

Early in the morning, Jesus stood on the shore, but the disciples did not recognise that it was Jesus. So, He called out to them, 'Children, do you have any fish?'

'No', they answered.

He told them, 'Cast the net on the right side of the boat, and you will find some.' So, they cast it there, and they were unable to haul it in because of the great number of fish.

Taken literally, there is absolutely no reason for such a story to appear in John's gospel, unless you want to believe that Jesus had an uncanny knack for knowing where to catch fish. But there is a deep lesson in this simple story.

The disciples are disheartened after Jesus' death. They have lost their way, their faith is diminished, and they have returned to their old habits, that is, allowing their left brain to dictate their actions. Left brain thinking – analysis, logic, reasoning – is not the way to higher consciousness. There is no love involved!

I'm not suggesting we do away with our left brain thought process. We need our left brain thinking to navigate through life. But the functions of the symbolic right brain hemisphere need to be tapped into for progression in the higher, spiritual realms.

Jesus tells the disciples, who haven't caught a fish all night, to go back in the water and cast their nets to the 'right'. As soon as they do this, their nets become so full of fish they struggle to pull them into the boat!

Do you see the symbolism here?

While fishing at night (darkness/the carnal mind) the disciples catch nothing. Christ (wisdom/light/illumination) appears to them in the early morning (Sunrise/the East) and instructs them to cast to the right (change their thinking from carnal mind to spiritual mind). As soon as the disciples change their way of thinking and use their spirit instead of their logic, they catch a boat load of fish!

Raise the spirit, raise the master

The lesson here is to employ the right-side functions of the brain. Don't neglect your intuition, insight, and holistic thought processes. But most of all, don't neglect love!

Christ represents higher consciousness and a higher you. This higher you – the ignition of your divine spark – cannot be achieved through scientific and mathematical processes, logic and concreteness.

You must employ your symbolic right-side brain functions. This involves tapping into the parasympathetic nervous system, which controls the body at rest, decreases the heart rate and restores the body to a state of calm. Meditation is a path to accessing the higher spiritual awareness of the right brain. Conversely the sympathetic nervous system of the left brain speeds up the body, causes tension and nervousness, and increases the heart rate.

The disciples lost their way because they were focused only on things they could see – the physical world. Christ (higher consciousness) had not appeared to them yet, so they lost their life's direction. But when they employed the right side of their brain (cast their net on the right) the rewards were abundant (all the fish).

Likewise, the grip of an Entered Apprentice and the grip of a Fellowcraft cannot raise GMHA from the grave, as both these grips represent left brain thinking. The Entered Apprentice grip represents the material aspects of the Entered Apprentice degree, which will not raise the Spirit. The Fellowcraft grip represents the science aspects of the Fellowcraft degree, which also will not raise the Spirit. Only when King Solomon taps into his higher, right brain functions is he capable of raising the body using the strength of the lion of the tribe of Judah, that is, through love. It is the power of love that raises the murdered intuitive power and divine self. Through love we raise our consciousness, and connect to the ultimate source of love, Supreme Consciousness.

As a man thinketh so he is, we're told in Proverbs 23:7.

Raise the spirit, raise the master.

Renew the mind

'Be ye transformed by the renewing of your mind,' we're told in Romans 14:17.

Look not at the things which are seen (the physical world) but at the things that are not seen (the Kingdom of Heaven within, the divine spark, your higher consciousness, your divine aspect).

The kingdom of heaven is not some far off place, it's a state of mind. This is why Freemasonry tells us it is the 'internal not the external qualifications of a man that Freemasonry regards'.

The Rose Croix 18th degree of Scottish Rite Masonry teaches that the letters INRI stand for: *Igne Natura Renovatur Integra* – All Nature is Renewed by Fire.

Pure matter is restored by spirit.

Our connection to the Centre is restored when we free ourselves of the chains of the material world (our crude nature/left brain functioning) and find the divine spark within. You become what you were intended to be – god-like. You don't become God, but god-like.

To free ourselves from our lower nature (the left side of the boat) we need to overcome our ego (left brain) and live in the spirit (right brain/right side of the boat). That's where we'll catch all the fish!

Lust, greed, adultery, sloth – that's all controlled by the left brain. We need to move our thought process (cast our net) from the left brain to the right brain. As King Solomon tells us, strength is located in the lion of the tribe of Judah, which camps on the East (right side/right brain).

The two hemispheres of the brain are also symbolised by the pillars of Boaz and Jachin. Though Boaz is said to be the left pillar and Jachin the right pillar, you must view them within yourself, visualising your brain as the temple. Therefore, Boaz is on your right (right hemisphere, intuitive, abstract, creative principle, higher spiritual nature) and Jachin on your left (left hemisphere, logic and intellect, physicality, concreteness).

Strength of the lion

King Solomon attempts to raise the body of GMHA by the Lion's Paw grip. The zodiac sign of the lion – Leo – symbolises the heart, which in turn is symbolic of love and strength. Interestingly, the astronomical sign of Leo actually looks like a cross-section of the human heart!

Only a strong heart – a heart the size of a lion – is capable of raising consciousness from earthly matter. Only pure love can raise the master from the trash of the ego's shackles.

Leo rules individualisation and initiation, where the soul and consciousness is recognised within the heart. Leo indicates the height of achievement of the human spirit, the spiritual goal of selflessness.

Out of the left brain

We are told in 2 Corinthians 3:6 that the scriptures should not be read literally. The same applies to Freemasonry.

King Solomon (wisdom) leads us out of our lower left brain and into our holistic, symbolic higher right brain. This is the process by which King Solomon raises the master from the grave.

This is also the process by which we can raise our own internal master.

Slowing the brain waves through meditation, sensory-deprivation or other methods causes the usually over-active left brain to ease off, allowing you greater access to the right hemisphere, or spiritual side, of the brain.

Only one who has overcome the trappings of the left brain is capable of raising the master. This is why the grip of an Entered Apprentice and the grip of a Fellowcraft fail to raise Grand Maser Hiram Abiff from the grave. This is also why the three ruffians are unable to gain the Master's Word from GMHA. They aren't qualified!

All the candidate in Freemasonry asks for is light. It should come as no surprise therefore that the Kingdom of Judah was known as the Kingdom of Light. And how about this for a kicker: Numbers 2:9 tells us that the camp of Judah comprised 186,400 people. Light in a vacuum travels at 186, 282 miles per second. The numbers are too close to be a coincidence! The Bible tells us the speed of light!

My mind is clear

The candidate in Freemasonry is always kept in the sunlight. He is never placed in the North of the lodge – the place of darkness. So long as the candidate stays in the symbolic light of the Sun, which represents goodness, knowledge, and higher learning, he will not err.

Knowledge is the 'power of the mind', and wisdom is the power of the mind to apply your knowledge at the right moment, at the right place and situation. Acting with wisdom brings us into harmony with ourselves, giving us a sense of self-worth and inner peace. This inner peace is achieved because we are acting in accordance with our conscience and avoiding the shame and guilt of following our baser instincts.

So long as you camp in the East like the tribe of Judah who held the banner of the lion, you will always be basked in light.

By employing the strength of the lion of the tribe of Judah – love/light/symbolic right brain – King Solomon raises the body of GMHA from the grave. Before doing so, however, he has an important dialogue with the Senior Grand Warden as they stand over the grave after failing to raise the body with the grips of an Entered Apprentice and a Fellowcraft.

King Solomon: Brother Senior Grand Warden, our attempts are in vain, what shall we do?

Senior Grand Warden: Let us pray.

Prayer is a form of meditation. It is an activity for stilling the mind, that is, quieting the clutter of the symbolic left brain. Through prayer/meditation – casting the net on the other side of the boat – those at the gravesite are able to still their minds and focus completely on the moment. They shift from symbolic left-brain function to right brain function, moving away from the earthly plane and touching the higher realm/spiritual plane.

At the conclusion of the prayer, the dialogue continues.

King Solomon: Brother Senior Grand Warden, your counsel was timely and good. Masons should ever remember that when the strength and wisdom of man fails, there is an inexhaustible supply above, yielded to us through the power of prayer. My mind is now clear, and the body shall be raised.

Here is King Solomon's big lesson for us: *My mind is now clear.* The body cannot be raised until the mind is clear! A state of higher consciousness and passage into the spiritual realms cannot be achieved until you clear your mind.

When the mind is stilled in meditation, the deep lying energy in the solar plexus travels up the nerve centres of the spine towards the brain. This has always been represented by the Sun rising after the winter solstice to sit at the East/right side/right brain on June 21, the summer solstice.

The symbology of clearing the mind is also evident in the divesting of the candidate of all metallic substances before entering the lodge room. In mythology, thought is represented by iron. Why? Because iron is heavy and weighs you down, just as thoughts are a heavy burden to carry. The divestment of all metallic substances teaches the candidate to clear his mind.

With a clear mind, that is, tapping into the symbolic right brain, King Solomon proceeds to raise the body of GMHA on the Five Points of Fellowship. To reiterate the importance of the symbolic right brain/right side/East a little more, the Five Points of Fellowship is completed by placing right on right:

- Right foot to right foot
- Right knee to right knee

- Right breast to right breast
- Right cheek to right cheek

The left hand is placed behind the back as we have no concern for what the left represents. This is the same reason why the first step taken by an Entered Apprentice is on the left foot. Stepping down on the left foot first, represents stepping down on all the left symbolises. Traditionally the left side of man symbolised evil, so stepping off on our left foot symbolises crushing evil thoughts and actions.

Interestingly, the Five Points of Fellowship when sketched looks like the Masonic square and compasses!

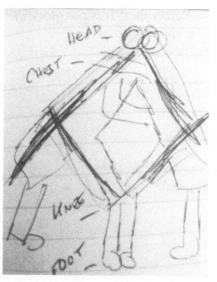

Author's sketch of the Five Points of Fellowship. Note how the positioning of the two bodies produces a representation of the Masonic square and compass.

A deep rabbit hole

There is an esoteric version of Freemasonry and an exoteric version. The exoteric version is what Albert Pike referred to as the 'outer court' in his book *Morals and Dogma*.

'The Blue degrees are but the outer court or portico of the Temple,' wrote Pike. 'Part of the symbols are displayed there to the Initiate, but he is intentionally misled by false interpretations. It is not intended that he shall understand them; but it is intended that he shall imagine he understands them. Their true explication is reserved for the Adepts, the Princes of Masonry.'

I don't believe Pike was entirely correct in his description of the blue degrees. The Entered Apprentice, Fellowcraft, and Master Mason degrees only remain the outer court of the Temple for those unwilling to look deeper. If you genuinely research the symbols and allegories of Freemasonry, as we are here, the treasure of the 'true explication' is attainable through the blue degrees.

The geniuses who penned Masonic ritual did not use Wikipedia directness. They offered up their secret wisdom, proven by the great sages, in the form of symbols and allegories which were to be taken as fiction outwardly but as a means of showing the profoundest truth and knowledge inwardly.

Remember: *It is the glory of God to conceal a thing, but it's the glory of a king to discover it.*

– 8 –
Brain Science

Freemasonry is brain science, and the ritual is a neurological handbook. The evidence is hidden in plain sight for those willing to look deeper than words on pages.

Our ceremonies, symbols and lectures are subtly focused on the brain, which is the hardware for the mind's software. Think of the brain as your body's central processing unit (CPU) that plays a key role in translating the content of your mind. It is the medium between our original spiritual state and our present physical manifestation.

Not convinced?

There are clues and signposts throughout Masonic ritual that tell us, without directly telling us, that Freemasonry is about the brain and the mind.

Clues and signposts

In the opening of the lodge we hear a description of the symbolic use of the Tyler's sword: 'To prevent the approach of every unworthy *thought*.'

This tells us in no uncertain terms that the job of the Tyler takes place in the brain! His job is to not prevent the approach of unworthy people, but of unworthy thoughts. You cannot cut, slice or stab a thought with a physical sword. Thoughts aren't material. They exist in, and emanate from, your brain.

Do you see?

Freemasonry is a system of self-improvement. It is about the brain, the mind, the spirit, and consciousness. Specifically, it is about raising consciousness, using the brain as the processing system by which to do so.

If you're not aspiring towards higher consciousness, which IS the ultimate goal of self-improvement, you're not really processing the Masonic intelligences passed down through the ages.

Writes Robert Lomas: 'The goal of all mystical attainment, whether in Masonry or elsewhere, is the union of the human with the divine consciousness.'[20] Such a union only happens when one achieves an elevation in consciousness.

The great Masonic author, WL Wilmshurst, wrote that the purpose of Freemasonry 'is to declare the way by which that [divine] centre may be found within ourselves, and this teaching is embodied in the discipline and ordeals delineated in the three degrees. No higher level of attainment is possible than that in which the human merges in the divine consciousness and knows as God knows.'[21]

Wilmshurst also wrote that initiation 'meant a process whereby natural man became transformed into spiritual or ultra-natural man, and to effect this it was necessary to change his consciousness, to gear it to a new and higher principle, and so, as it were, make of him a new man in the sense of attaining a new method of life and a new outlook upon the universe.'[22]

Freemasonry is the modern incarnation of the ancient mystery schools which focused on the brain and mind as the means to free higher consciousness from the shackles of ego.

Let's look closer at the brain and the mind, and how they correspond to Masonic teaching.

The most amazing place in the universe
The most amazing place in the universe is your brain.

The brain is composed of a set of four interconnected cavities (ventricles) where cerebrospinal fluid (CSF) is produced. Within each ventricle is a region of choroid plexus, a network of ependymal cells involved in the production of CSF.

The four ventricles are: two lateral ventricles, the third ventricle, and the fourth ventricle.

The fourth ventricle is located closest to the spine and is considered almost as an entry to the brain. Therefore, it can be said to be the 'ground floor' of the ventricular system.

As the ground floor, the fourth ventricle correlates with the Entered Apprentice degree, as one is made an Entered Apprentice 'in a place representing the ground floor of King Solomon's Temple.'

The fourth ventricle is characteristically diamond-shaped in cross-section. It bears a striking resemblance to the Masonic square and compasses. The flattened square and compasses (diamond) shaped cavity of the hindbrain contains cerebrospinal fluid and is continuous with the cerebral aqueduct through the third ventricle.

The lateral ventricles are the largest in the series of four interconnecting fluid-filled cavities and form a C shape within the brain. The letter C is a shape that winds. The lateral ventricles represent the Middle Chamber of the Fellowcraft degree, complete with a winding staircase in the shape of the letter C.

The third ventricle is situated in the middle of the cerebral hemispheres between the right and left lateral ventricles. It is bounded by the thalamus and hypothalamus on both the left and right sides. The lamina terminalis forms the anterior wall. The floor is formed by hypothalamic structures. The roof is formed by the ependyma, lining the undersurface of the *tela choroidea* of the third ventricle.

The third ventricle really is a small room in the middle of your brain. It is also the location of the pineal gland. As such it represents the Master Mason degree and the sanctum sanctorum of King Solomon's temple. The pineal gland is activated by light, which is all a Mason ever asks for in any of the degrees.

The pineal gland

To activate the pineal gland is to come face to face with your own divinity. This is what happened when Jacob wrestled God through the night.

This well-known Biblical story is not about a physical wrestling match, but Jacob wrestling against his carnal desires, his animal nature.

Jacob's problem had always been his dependence on his material and carnal desires (symbolic left brain) instead of trusting his higher self; his spiritual nature (symbolic right brain). Jacobs wrestles God through the night until his femur is put out. God asks the injured Jacob to let Him go and Jacob refuses to do so unless He blesses him. God blesses Jacob and Jacob names the place where he was blessed Peniel, which translates as 'Face of God'. God also gives Jacob a new name, Israel.

Peniel looks like pineal, right? The pineal gland is said to be the seat of the soul and the means by which we connect to our spiritual self – the means by which we can see the face of God.

Jacob saw the face of God, that is, he saw his own divinity and came together with God in the pineal gland of his brain. The moment Jacob became Israel is the moment he transmuted/alchemized himself and became enlightened. It's the moment he camped at the symbolic East.

When you understand that the sanctum sanctorum of King Solomon's Temple is a symbol for the brain's third ventricle containing the pineal gland, you better comprehend why we are told that Grand Master Hiram Abiff (GMHA) retreated to the sanctum sanctorum every day at noon (the sun at its meridian/light at its highest point) to pray (clear his mind/go inside himself/meditate/stimulate his pineal gland).

Whenever we read about GMHA praying, we are actually reading about him meditating.

Is there a difference between prayer and meditation?

Prayer is a method of the individual seeking and conversing with Supreme Consciousness/God/Universal Mind/the Source. Meditation is a method of allowing Supreme Consciousness/God/Universal Mind/the Source to speak to us.

The pineal gland is a light receptor, and if God (Supreme Consciousness) is Light, as the Bible constantly tells us, then the pineal gland is our God receptor.

The pineal gland is a photosensitive organ that knows day from night. It is the production centre for melatonin, which is released in the dark, during sleep, and has been linked to spiritual experience as it quiets the body and mind, allowing access to higher consciousness.

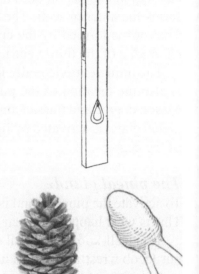

The plumb line with its suspended pinecone / the pinecone / the pinecone shaped pineal gland

The pineal gland is stimulated during meditation, but such meditation should take place in the dark to enable greater melatonin secretion. Melatonin flowing from the pineal gland requires an absence of light. This is where we get the saying 'from darkness, light'. It is also one of the reasons why the candidate for Freemasonry is kept in the dark for so long before being brought to light in each of the three degrees.

The Bible tells us that in order to achieve a state of higher consciousness, and experience Supreme Consciousness (God), one should meditate in the dark to activate the reception of light via the pineal.

Psalms 18:11: 'He made darkness his secret place.'

Amos 5:18: 'Woe unto you that desire the day of the LORD! to what end is it for you? the day of the LORD is darkness, and not light.'

Matthew 4:16: 'The people who sat in darkness saw great light.'

Matthew 6:6: 'But you, when you pray enter into your closet and when you have shut the door, pray to your Father which is in secret; and your Father which sees in secret shall reward you openly.'

In the darkened sanctum sanctorum, GMHA's thoughts centre on his symbolic right brain, that is his higher spiritual side. He has entered his closet and shut the door. As such his pineal gland is activated and he achieves a higher state of consciousness (your Father which sees in secret shall reward you openly).

Inside the holy of holies GMHA is away from the profane workmen who are outside the temple. Only when GMHA leaves the sanctum sanctorum – when his mind travels back down to a lower state; symbolic left brain thinking – is he accosted by the three ruffians, that is by carnal desire and the physical realm, which leads to death.

Consciousness, the pineal gland and the candidate for Freemasonry

You are consciousness. Consciousness remembers when not attached to a physical brain. But when consciousness is attached to a physical brain, it submits to the physical control and then only remembers when the brain allows it to do so.

This control is exerted by symbolic left-brain functioning. In the holy of holies each day, GMHA detaches his consciousness from the symbolic left brain and casts his net to the right by stilling his mind through prayer (meditation).

The pineal gland is located at the geometric centre of your brain. It moderates your wake-sleep patterns and circadian rhythms, remains uniquely isolated from the blood-brain barrier system (GMHA isolated in prayer/meditation, away from the profane), and receives a higher percentage of blood flow than any other area of the body, save the kidneys. It is activated by light and is considered the most powerful and highest source of ethereal energy available to humans.

The pineal gland is formed in the human embryo after forty-nine days – the same amount of time Tibetans believe it takes for the reincarnation of a human soul. It is also the same amount of time that the human embryo becomes either male or female.

The candidate for Freemasonry is representative of the pineal gland.

Once again, all the candidate ever asks for is light, more light and further light in Freemasonry.

Why does he only ask for light?

Light stimulates the pineal gland. Stimulating the pineal gland activates the third eye. The candidate in Freemasonry seeks to ignite his divine spark!

As mentioned above, the pineal gland receives more blood flow per cubic area than any other gland in your body. In other words, compared to all your other organs, this tiny gland gets the highest concentration of energy. Similarly, during initiation, the energy of the entire lodge and its officers is focused solely on the candidate.

The purpose of Freemasonry, and therefore the purpose of the candidate, is to re-energise the body, the glands, the nerve centres, the brain, etc., and re-activate the dormant pineal gland (inner spiritual eye) to ignite the divine spark. Ignition of the divine spark brings about a higher state of consciousness, placing us in closer contact with Supreme Consciousness (God/The Universal Mind).

The lodge as the brain

Officers of the lodge represent parts of the brain.

As the ritual states, the lodge room is an oblong shape, not a square or a circle. This is because the head/brain is not round, but most resembles the form of an oblong.

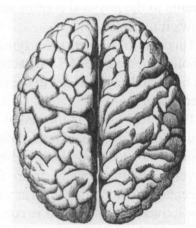

The two Deacons represent the two hemispheres of the brain that are under the control of the physical nature (Senior Warden), the intellectual nature (the Worshipful Master) and the emotional nature (Junior Warden).

As with most Buddhist temples, Masonic lodge rooms (temples) look like an esoteric map of the brain. The North of the lodge, a place of darkness where nothing of great

The oblong brain, just as the lodge room is always oblong shape.

importance takes place, is devoid of any principal officers. The greatest action in the lodge happens on the right side of the room, representative of the right side of the brain.

I won't detail every lodge officer's position and how they correspond to the various parts of the brain, but let's examine some of the more obvious connections.

The Tyler is the Brain Stem. It is the Tyler's duty to observe the approach of Cowans and eavesdroppers and suffer none to pass or re-pass except such as are duly qualified and have permission from the Worshipful Master.

The Tyler guards the outer door of the lodge. Symbolically, he is the guardian of your thoughts. You should employ your personal Tyler to permit entrance into your brain only those thoughts that are 'duly qualified,' that is, positive thoughts.

The jewel of the Tyler's office is a sword, and if one looks at a picture of the brain atop the brain stem, it resembles an orb atop a sword.

The brain stem includes the midbrain, pons and medulla. It acts as a relay centre connecting the cerebrum and the cerebellum to the spinal cord.

Do you see the connection with the Tyler?

His duty is to act as a relay centre between the outside world and lodge room.

The brain stem is located at the back of the brain, which if you picture the brain as an oblong lodge room, places the Tyler in the West, as he should be.

Almost all sensory neurons of the spinal cord send atoms up to the thalamus for processing. Located at the top of the brain stem (near the Tyler), the thalamus acts as a two-way relay station, sorting, processing and directing signals from the spinal cord and mid-brain (Tyler) structures to the cerebrum; and conversely from the cerebrum down the spinal cord to the nervous system.

This processing is done before any information is passed onwards to your sensory cortex bits at which point you become consciously aware of that sensory input. Similarly, it is only through the Junior Deacon's attendance to alarms from the Tyler that the lodge becomes aware of information from the outside.

The jewel of the Junior Deacon is a dove bearing an olive branch. The thalamus, which corresponds to the Junior Deacon, is oval in shape and most often described as resembling a dove's egg.

The hippocampus of the brain sends out memories to the appropriate part of the cerebral hemisphere for long-term storage and retrieves them when necessary.

In other words, the hippocampus makes a record of all that happens. This brain part relates directly to the Secretary of the lodge whose duty is to observe the proceedings of the lodge and make a full record of all that is proper to be written. It is the Secretary's job, as is the job of the hippocampus, to record memories.

The jewel of the Secretary's Office is the crossed quills, and if one looks at a picture of the hippocampus of the brain, it resembles two crossed quills.

The Junior Warden sits in the South, or midway position in the lodge. It is his duty to observe the sun at its meridian, which is the glory and beauty of the day; to call the Craft from labour to refreshment and superintend them during the hours thereof, carefully to observe that the means of refreshment are not perverted to intemperance or excess, and see that they return to their labours in due season, that the Worshipful Master may receive honour and they pleasure and profit thereby.

The Junior Warden is all about the regulation of pleasure and refreshment and rewarding the Craftsmen for their hard work. This corresponds to the role of dopamine, a chemical in your brain that affects your emotions, movements and your sensations of pleasure and pain. It is commonly known as the body's 'reward' chemical.

Dopamine is involved many different pathways of the brain, but most of us associate it with the mesolimbic pathway, which starts with the cells in the ventral tegmental area, buried deep in the middle of the brain (just as the Junior Warden is situated in the mid-line of the lodge, between the Worshipful Master and the Senior Warden).

During the dramatisation of the legend of the third degree, GMHA represents the Junior Warden. It is the Junior Warden's jewel (the plumb line) that is found around GMHA's neck. As the Junior Warden, GMHA here represents the pineal gland.

The Junior Warden represents the sun at its meridian when the greatest amount of light is cast upon the largest area of the earth's surface. The pineal gland is activated by light and is considered the most powerful and highest source of ethereal energy available to humans, thus corresponding with the sun at its meridian. The pineal gland is located in the middle of the brain, just as the Junior Warden is located in the middle of the lodge room.

Two of the most important parts of the brain are the hypothalamus and the pituitary gland.

The hormones of the pituitary gland help regulate the functions of other endocrine glands, namely the thyroid gland, adrenal gland, ovaries and testes. Though it is often referred to as the 'master gland,' the pituitary gland isn't necessarily the boss. That distinction belongs to the

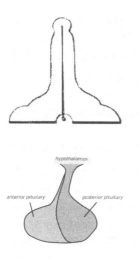

Some Masonic working tools and jewels closely resemble the parts of the brain to which they correspond, such as the Senior Warden's Level, which resembles the pituitary gland, which is the Senior Warden of the brain.

hypothalamus which signals the pituitary to stimulate or inhibit hormone production. Essentially, the pituitary acts after prompting from the hypothalamus.[23]

The hypothalamus has been described as 'the magic centimetre at the centre of the brain…the driver of the body,'[24] If the hypothalamus is healthy, then you are healthy, and if it is not there are very dangerous consequences.

The overall role of the hypothalamus and the pituitary is to monitor and make sure that the whole of the body is in harmony.

What is the duty of the Senior Warden? To oversee the craftsmen while at labour and ensure the harmony of the lodge.

What is the duty of the Worshipful Master? To set the craft at work, giving them proper instruction for their labours.

The hypothalamus gives instruction to the pituitary gland. It is the master gland; the control centre of the entire body. Attached to the roof of the third ventricle, it continuously receives information on the status of the

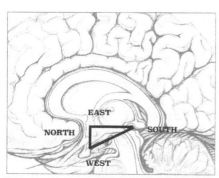

The brain as the lodge room. The Three points of the triangle are the location of the pineal gland (SOUTH), hypothalamus (EAST) and the pituitary gland (WEST). They correspond to the three principal officers of the lodge: Worshipful Master (EAST), Senior Warden (WEST) and Junior Warden (SOUTH).

body systems via nerve impulses, just as the Worshipful Master receives information on the status of the lodge via his various officers. The hypothalamus interprets messages, evaluates them, and dispatches outgoing messages via nerves/hormones.

The hypothalamus represents the Worshipful Master of the lodge. The pituitary regulates the work of all endocrine glands and thus represents the Senior Warden whose duty is to regulate the workmen of the Temple – to supervise the craftsmen at work.

The three principal officers of the lodge form a triangle within the lodge room, with the Worshipful Master and Senior Warden opposite one another, and the Junior Warden in the centre. Likewise, in the brain, the hypothalamus (Worshipful Master) is situated opposite the pituitary (Senior Warden) with the pineal gland (Junior Warden) between the two, forming a triangle. The brain stem (Tyler) is located in the West next to the pituitary (Senior Warden), as in the lodge room.

The meditation processes of Universal Healing Tao centres around the jobs of three specific brain parts: the hypothalamus (our Worshipful Master); the pineal gland (our Junior Warden); and the pituitary gland (our Senior Warden). The pineal gland connects us to the Universal Energy during meditation. From the hypothalamus we project our spirit upwards and receive the descending Universal Energy. The pituitary gland receives the Cosmic Force used to launch the spirit bodies into the earthly or human plan for traveling. These deepest centres in the brain are activated in relationship to Spirit.[25]

The jewels worn by the three principal officers also bear a striking resemblance to their corresponding brain parts.

WORSHIPFUL MASTER
The Square
Hypothalamus

SENIOR WARDEN
The Level
Pituitary

JUNIOR WARDEN
The Plumb Rule
Pineal

The representation of the pineal gland is quite clearly seen in the Junior Warden's jewel of the plumb rule. There is no doubt that the plumb bob's pinecone shape represents the pinecone shape of the pineal gland, corresponding to the Junior Warden.

How did the ritual writers possibly know so much about the brain? Surely the functions of specific parts of the brain such as the hippocampus, hypothalamus and ventral tegmental are the discoveries of modern neuroscience?

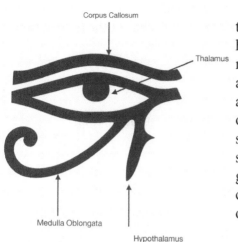

Corpus Callosum

Thalamus

Medulla Oblongata

Hypothalamus

The Ancient Egyptian Eye of Horus, bears a striking resemblance to the centre of the brain in cross section.

Old Kingdom Egyptian medical texts speak of the brain having hemispheres and being enclosed in a membrane; the ancient Egyptians also performed brain surgery. The ancient Egyptian symbol of the Eye of Horus looks exactly like a cross-section of the human brain, distinctly showing the thalamus, pituitary gland, pineal gland, cerebellum, corpus callosum, and medulla oblongata.

Fast forward to the 1400s and Leonardo da Vinci's pioneering research into the brain that led him to discoveries in neuroanatomy and neurophysiology. His injection of hot wax into the brain of an ox provided a cast of the ventricles and represents the first known use of a solidifying medium to define the shape and model of sensory physiology. He undertook his research with the broad goal of providing physical explanations of how the brain processes visual and other sensory input and integrates that information via the soul.

The brain is the temple

King Solomon's Temple is not a literal temple. As the ritual clearly states, it is a house not made with hands, eternal in the heavens, not eternal on the Earth. The ritual writers are clearly telling us that their use of the Temple building is symbolic and allegorical.

We are told that it took three Grand Masters, 3,300 masters or overseers of the work, 80,000 Fellowcrafts and 70,000 Entered Apprentices to build the temple. This is a ludicrous number of workmen for the construction of any building, especially when you consider that the Empire State building was built in only one year and 45 days, using 3,000 workers.

So why did the ritual writers use such specific and large numbers in the allegory of the temple's construction?

What do these numbers really mean?

The number of workers employed in the building of the temple represents the workings of the spine and brain as they relate to the body's nervous system and energy flow.

The Masonic ritual writers really were geniuses!

The Three Grand Masters symbolise the three areas of the human brain:
- Forebrain
- Midbrain
- Hindbrain

They also symbolise the threefold make-up of a human being:
- Mind/Soul
- Body
- Spirit

The 3,300 masters or overseers of the work are broken down as thus:

$3300 = 3+3+0+0 = 6$ – represents the six regions of the brain:
- Diencephalon
- Mesencephalon
- Pons
- Cerebellum
- Medulla Oblongata

The brain is also divided into these 6 major parts:

1. Lobes of the brain:
- Frontal Lobes
- Temporal Lobes
- Occipital Lobes
- Parietal Lobes

2. Motor Cortex

3. Brain Stem

4. The Limbic System
- The Thalamus
- The Hypothalamus
- The Hippocampus
- The Amygdala

5. Cerebrum

6. Cerebellum

The 3,300 masters or overseers of the work also represents the 33 vertebrae of the spine, which is the body's pathway to the brain.

The 80,000 Fellowcrafts represent the 31 pairs of spinal nerves being:

31 x 2 (pairs) = 62
6 + 2 = 8
8 = 80,000 as 8+0+0+0+0

There were 31 chambers in King Solomon's Temple, representing the 31 pairs of spinal nerves. There were also three levels in King Solomon's Temple, just as there are three levels of brain function: the medulla, the sub cortical and the cortex area. There are also three parts of the brain: the forebrain, the midbrain and the hindbrain.

The 70,000 Entered Apprentices symbolise the seven chakras.

Chakras are centres in our body through which energy flows. The seven chakras and their locations are as follows:

• Root chakra – Base of spine in tailbone area.
• Sacral chakra – Lower abdomen, about two inches below the navel and two inches in.
• Solar Plexus chakra – Upper abdomen in the stomach area.
• Heart chakra – Centre of chest just above the heart.
• Throat chakra – Throat.
• Third eye chakra – Forehead between the eyes (also called the Brow Chakra).
• Crown chakra – The top of the head.

The number 7 also symbolises the seven principles that comprise a human being, as detailed in the teachings of Theosophy, a system of esoteric philosophy concerning, or investigation seeking direct knowledge of, presumed mysteries of being and nature, especially about the nature of divinity.

The teachings of Theosophy became popular in the 1800s – also a time for the writing and development of much of the current Masonic ritual.

According to the teachings of Theosophy, human beings comprise seven principles, divided into a Higher Triad and a Lower Quaternary, or 3+4 (7). The higher triad lasts forever, whereas the lower quaternary lasts just one lifetime.

Masonic ritual tells us that King Solomon's Temple was supported by 1453 columns and 2906 pilasters. These numbers break down as such:

1453 columns = 1+4+5+3 = 13; 1+3 = 4

2906 pilasters = 2+9+0+6 = 17; 1+7 = 8
4 (columns) + 8 (pilasters) = 12
12 = 1+2 = 3
3 supports of the Temple!
1. Beauty
2. Strength
3. Wisdom

1. The Worshipful Master
2. Senior Warden
3. Junior Warden

1. Mind (Soul)
2. Body
3. Spirit

1. Midbrain
2. Forebrain
3. Hindbrain

1. Lower Body (feet to abdomen)
2. Mid Body (abdomen to neck)
3. Upper Body (neck to head)

Ritual tells us that the columns and pilasters were 'hewn from the finest Parian marble.'

Parian marble is the famous marble of Paros, Greece. It was used for the construction of the Acropolis, the temple of Zeus in Olympia, the temple of Apollo in Delphi, the temple of Apollo Epicurus in Peloponnese and in almost all the great temples and sanctuaries. Famous statues were also made of Parian marble, including the Venus de Milo, Hermes of Praxitelis and the Victory of Samothrace.[26]

What's so special about Parian marble? Its main characteristics are clearness, limpidness, and its ability to capture light!

Once again, we see that there is nothing of insignificance in Masonic ritual. Everything contributes towards Freemasonry's main purpose – the attainment of light!

The three Grand Masters who oversaw the building of the Temple were: King Solomon

King Hiram of Tyre
Grand Master Hiram Abiff

They represent the three supports of the Temple (the Temple being you). They are mind (soul), body and spirit.

King Solomon could not build the temple by himself. He needed the support of Hiram, King of Tyre and GMHA. When these three join forces – Mind (Soul), Body, Spirit – the Temple is built.

King Solomon is the SPIRIT: He conceives the temple and gives the workmen proper instructions for their labours.

King Hiram of Tyre is the BODY: He provides the physical materials for the temple.

GMHA is the MIND (SOUL): He beautifies the temple, just as the mind (soul) beautifies the human being. (A Beautiful Mind/Beautiful Soul)

These three together possess the LOST WORD which, the Bible tells us, was with God in the beginning and the Word was God. When GMHA dies, the Word is lost. Why? Because without the Soul/Mind (GMHA), the Spirit (King Solomon) and the Body (King Hiram of Tyre) have no union. Without any one of these three, we are incomplete.

The Lost Word is the combination of the MIND, BODY and SPIRIT. All three together allow a connection to the Source, to Supreme Consciousness, to the divine spark.

Amazing, isn't it?

Coded into the number of workmen employed in the building of King Solomon's Temple is a blueprint for the human brain, nervous system and chakra points, and the key to understanding the Lost Word of a Master Mason, which is the balance of mind, body and spirit.

Timbers of Lebanon

Masonic ritual is specific about what materials were used in the construction of the Temple and from where these materials were taken.

'The stones were hewn, squared, and numbered in the quarries where raised; the timbers felled and prepared in the forests of Lebanon, conveyed by sea in floats to Joppa, and thence by land to Jerusalem.'

Joppa and Lebanon have deep symbolic significance.

After the three ruffians killed GMHA, they left the temple at Jerusalem and traveled in a Westward direction (opposite the East, away from wisdom, light, higher consciousness), towards the port of Joppa.

Joppa symbolises a pathway to higher consciousness. The ruffians were attempting to attain passage to a higher state but were not qualified to receive such passage.

Scripture tells us that Jonah set out from Joppa (higher consciousness) to Tarshish (lower consciousness) to escape the presence of the Lord. In other words, he tried to escape his higher nature to his lower nature.

Jonah was thrown from the boat into the sea. Instead of drowning, God rescued him by providing a sea monster to swallow him. Jonah repented and prayed for three days while in the body of the sea monster (went inside himself/cleared his mind/meditation) and was thrown up onto the shores of Nineveh.

Lebanon symbolises the body, and it was there that the physical material – wood – was taken for the building of the temple.

The name Lebanon comes from the root verb 'Laben' meaning to become white. Also, the feminine noun 'Lebanah,' which means 'brick'. The denominative verb 'Laban' means to 'make bricks'. Lebanon is clearly all about the physical.

The wood derived from Lebanon was specifically cedar wood. The cedar tree is an evergreen plant, the male cone of which curves like a human spine, on top of which you will find pinecones. Pinecones have long symbolised the pineal gland due to their shape.

The wood of the cedar is peculiarly adapted to building because it is not subject to decay, nor to being eaten by worms or other pests. Its wood is red in colour, solid, beautiful to the eye and free of knots.

In Ezekiel's writings, God says of the cedar tree: 'A tree so tall it reaches the clouds. Its roots reached down to the deep-flowing streams. I made it beautiful, with spreading branches, it was the envy of every tree in Eden, the garden of God.'

So, the evergreen (immortal) cedar tree, which grows in the shape of a human spine with nerves branching off on all sides, and produces red (blood) wood, is taken from Lebanon (the body) and transported by floats to Joppa (gateway to higher consciousness) and then onto Jerusalem (higher consciousness).

The banks of the River Jordan

Masonic ritual tells us that the pillars of the temple, Boaz and Jachin, 'were cast in the clay grounds on the banks of the River Jordan, between Succoth and Zeredatha, where King Solomon ordered these and all the sacred vessels of the Temple to be cast. They were cast hollow for the purpose of containing the rolls and records which composed the archives of our ancient Brethren.'

Let's look closer at the symbolism of the River Jordan and why, specifically, the pillars were cast there in the clay grounds.

The River Jordan is about 200 miles long. It lies in a structural depression and has the lowest elevation of any river in the world. The river rises on the slopes of Mount Hermon, on the border between Syria and Lebanon, and flows southward through northern Israel to the Sea of Galilee (Lake Tiberius). Exiting the sea, it continues south, dividing Israel and the Israeli-occupied West Bank to the West from Jordan to the East before emptying into the Dead Sea. The surface of the Dead Sea, at an elevation of about 1,410 feet (430 metres) below sea level is the lowest land point on Earth.[27] The Jordan River has three principal sources, all of which rise at the foot of Mount Hermon.

The River Jordan is significant for Jews because the tribes of Israel under Joshua crossed the river on dry ground to enter the Promised Land after years of wandering in the desert.

The desert wandering, of course, took place after hundreds of years of enslavement in Egypt. Exodus 12:40 tells us: 'Now the sojourning of the children of Israel who dwelt in Egypt, was four hundred and thirty years.'

430 years = 4+3+0 = 7

The number 7 symbolises rising up through the seven chakras, which is necessary for attainment of higher consciousness.

The same path through the seven chakras to the attainment of higher consciousness is contained within the officers' line of the Masonic lodge. If one joins the officers' line as a Junior Steward, it takes seven years to become Worshipful Master:

1st year – Junior Steward – root chakra
2nd year – Senior Steward – sacral chakra
3rd year – Junior Deacon – solar plexus chakra
4th year – Senior Deacon – heart chakra
5th year – Junior Warden – throat chakra
6th year – Senior Warden – Third Eye chakra
7th year – Worshipful Master – Crown Chakra

Crown
Third Eye
Throat
Heart
Solar Plexus
Sacral
Root

In many Masonic jurisdictions, the Worshipful Master wears a hat. This is symbolic of his having achieved activation of the seventh or Crown Chakra, which sits, as a hat, atop the head.

We must look at these stories allegorically. As such, crossing the river on dry ground to the Promised Land represents the Jewish people achieving a higher level of consciousness, a state of being of which they were devoid whilst wandering in the desert.

The River Jordan is symbolic of the spine. The spine leads to the brain. The brain consists of three parts, hence the three principal sources from which the river flows, all of which rise at the foot of Mount Hermon, that is, all of which emanate from the brain (Mount Hermon).

Allegorically, Joshua led the tribes of Israel across the Jordan into the Promised Land of milk and honey. The symbolism here is that after being enslaved by the Egyptians (enslaved by the ego/lower self/no connection to the Universal Mind) the Jewish people wandered in the desert (barren wasteland/devoid of higher consciousness) until such time as Joshua (meaning 'Salvation') led them across the River Jordan (the spine) to the Promised Land (the symbolic right brain/higher consciousness/ reconnection to the Universal Mind).

The Promised Land flowed with milk and honey. This is strictly symbolic. The Promised Land is the brain; the milk is the white substance DMT secreted by the pineal gland during deep meditation. Honey is the yellow (or gold) of the seven key hormones secreted by the pituitary gland that are related to lactation, the release of testosterone, and the production of sex, thyroid, and human growth hormones.

The brain, specifically the right side of the brain, is the Promised Land. It is here that we reconnect with God/Universal Mind/Supreme Consciousness.

In the section of the Masonic Ritual under our present study, clay is of the earth, which represents man, or more specifically the flesh of man. The River Jordan represents spinal fluid in the spinal canal. The body's energy rises from the sacrum (the Dead Sea; one end of the River Jordan) up the human spinal canal, all the way to the brain (Mt Hermon; the other end of the River Jordan with its three sources, or three parts of the brain).

The two pillars Boaz and Jachin represent both the channels on either side of the spine (ida and pingala, left and right) through which flow the energies of the physical body, subtle body and causal body.

Jachin and Boaz

The symbolism of two pillars/columns is not unique to Freemasonry. Hermes Trismegistus concealed the knowledge of the antediluvian world in two pillars. One contained Art (the right brain) and the other contained Science (the left brain).

The pillars of Solomon's Temple, we are told, were cast hollow for the purpose of containing the 'rolls and records which composed the archives of our ancient Brethren'.

Once again, we are not meant to take 'rolls and records' literally. What would be the point of keeping rolls and records of ancient Brethren? A list of old names is useless in a system of self-improvement.

'Rolls and records' are symbolic of the real information stored in the pillars – DNA, the strands of which takes the shape of a winding staircase.

DNA has been described as a tape recorder of your complete ancestry. It is a record book of your genetic code, the carrier of genetic information. However, we have not unlocked all the information contained within our DNA – nowhere close to it! Masonic ritual tells us that if we are able to tap into the 'rolls and records' of our ancient Brethren – the secrets of the world – we can raise our consciousness and access the complete resources of our DNA. Information about who we are and why we are and where we came from will not appear from an outside source. It is already in our DNA!

Just as Hermes Trismegistus placed all the knowledge of the world inside two pillars, so all the knowledge of the world is inside our own pillars. It's in our DNA! It's in our brain. We just need the find the means to access it, and that is done by raising consciousness.

'The rolls and records which composed the archives of our ancient Brethren' is a reference to our DNA. Even the numbers add up to this conclusion.

We know that the pillars represent the spinal cord because the pillars stood 18 cubits high, and the human spinal cord is 18 inches long. The chapiters atop the pillars were 5 cubits in size, and the human brain is 5 inches wide. The human spinal cord is hollow with a circumference of 12mm (cross sectional area of spinal cord at C2 level), and Boaz and Jachin were hollow pillars with a circumference of 12 cubits.

The pillars stood 18 cubits with chapiters of 5 cubits.

18+5 = 23

The human genome of Homo Sapiens is stored on 23 chromosome pairs.

These measurements are not a coincidence.

Once again we see the genius of the Masonic ritual writers to hide such information in plain sight hundreds of years before the 'DNA discoveries' of James Watson and Francis Crick in the 1950s.

The pillars also represent the fornix of the brain, which makes sense when you understand that the pillars carry DNA. The fornix is the major output tract of the hippocampus. They are almost always described as 'columns' and 'pillars'.

The columns of the fornix (anterior pillars; fornicolumns) arch downward and descend through the grey matter in the lateral wall of the third ventricle, which as previously mentioned is the location of the pineal gland, or the Sanctum Sanctorum of the Temple. Like Boaz and Jachin, the columns/pillars of the fornix act as the columns/pillars of the body's Temple.

The *crura*, or posterior pillars/columns of the fornix are, at their beginning, connected with the under surface of the corpus callosum, which is the area that allows communication between the two hemispheres of the brain – symbolised by walking between the two pillars of Boaz and Jachin.

One of the functions of the fornix is to connect the hippocampus to the mammillary bodies of the hypothalamus. As we know, the hippocampus is where our memories are stored, hence the connection between DNA within the pillars being the 'rolls and records' mentioned in Masonic ritual.

Do you see how it all comes together?

Boaz and Jachin contain our DNA record, which is attached to our memories of who we are and where we came from.

It's all about brain function!

We are flesh (clay grounds) containing incredible energy. The energy rises from the solar plexus (Dead Sea), via the spinal fluid through the spine (the River Jordan), and passes through the fornix (two pillars) to activate the pineal gland (holy of holies). This is the building of the Temple, which took seven years to complete (energy must pass through the seven chakras). The pineal gland (Peniel) is where we come face to face with God (our higher consciousness/connection with Supreme Consciousness).

If you don't yet believe Freemasonry is about elevating your consciousness from lower to higher, here's another kicker for you.

We know that the pillars Boaz and Jachin measured 18 cubits in height.

18 is 1+8 = 9

The number 9 has tremendous symbolic value attached to it.

- 9 is the number of consciousness in Greek.
- 9 is the number of waking human consciousness in ancient mythology.
- A full circle with no beginning and no end represents God/Supreme Consciousness. If you bisect a circle ($360° – 3+6+0 = 9$) you get $180°$ ($1+8+0 = 9$). Bisect that again and you get $90°$ ($9+0 = 9$). Bisect that again and you get $45°$ ($4+5 = 9$). Bisected again you get $22.5°$ ($2+2+5 = 9$). Truly Supreme Consciousness is everywhere, from the largest circle to the small bisection!
- An equilateral triangle, which symbolises the perfect harmony of mind – body – spirit contains three angles of $60°$, which is $6+6+6 = 18 – 1+8 = 9$.
- In numerology, 9 is Universal love, eternity, Universal Spiritual Laws, Spiritual Enlightenment, Spiritual Awakening, a Higher Perspective.

15 days in the grave

Ritual tells us that GMHA's body had been in the grave for 15 days before it was discovered. Fifteen days equals:

15 x 24 (hours) = 360 - 3+6 = 9

Let's consider, for a moment, the chronology of events surrounding the discovery of GMHA's body.

The body is found after being dead for 15 days. News of the discovered body is reported to King Solomon. King Solomon then sends the Fellowcrafts to the gravesite to discover any word or jewel attached to GMHA's body. The Fellowcrafts remove the Junior Warden's jewel from GMHA's body and return it to King Solomon.

King Solomon then takes the Grand Senior Warden and the entire Craft on a procession to the grave of GMHA where he is symbolically raised.

If the Fellowcrafts reported their discovery of GMHA's body 15 days after his death, it is safe to assume that the procession to the grave and subsequent raising of GMHA was performed on the sixteenth day of his death, having been dead for 15 days. The number 16 gives us a symbolic $1+6 = 7$; the seven chakras to higher consciousness.

Knowing as we do that Freemasonry is a collection of teachings from various ancient mystery schools and religious systems, it is interesting to note that in Hinduism the final *sanskara* (sacraments of life from conception to death) is performed on the sixteenth day after death. This is known as the Antyeshti Sanskara.

Sanskara are rites of passage in a human being's life described in ancient Sanskrit texts, as well as a concept in the karma theory of Indian philosophies. The word literally means 'putting together, making perfect, getting ready, to prepare,' or 'a sacred or sanctifying ceremony' in ancient Sanskrit and Pali texts of India.

That powerful number 9
Let's explore this all-important number 9 a little more.

In Acts 3:6 (3+6 = 9) the command is given to the lame man to 'Rise up and walk!'

Symbolically the man is not physically lame but spiritually lame. He resides only in his lower self. He thought money was the greatest need in his life. He never gave thought to anything but accumulating money through begging at the gate of the Temple (outside the Temple/outside of his higher consciousness).

When the man is commanded to 'Rise up and walk!' in the name of Jesus Christ (higher consciousness), he does so. It takes effort for the lame man to rise up and finally walk (connect with his spiritual side). It's not easy to detach from one's lower nature/ego/lust/animal side. No one else helps the lame man rise, he must do it himself, as must we all.

The lame man had the ability to rise up (access his higher self) inside him all the time, but his ego never allowed him to see the pathway to his higher self.

We too need to 'rise up and walk!'

The symbolism of 9 is also seen in the lodge room.

When the Worshipful Master opens a lodge, he symbolically raises the consciousness of all present. To complete the lodge's opening, he tells the Junior Deacon to inform the Tyler that the lodge is opened. The Junior Deacon knocks on the door three times (XXX), followed by three knocks from the Tyler (XXX), followed by three more knocks from the Junior Deacon (XXX).

3 + 3 + 3 = 9

During circumambulation of the Brother for the third degree, the three Principal Officers deliver a total of nine knocks of their gavels as the Brother passes before them.

Next time you sit in lodge, pay notice to how many 3 x 3s occur. It's all about attaining higher consciousness!

Duality of Boaz and Jachin

The pillars Boaz and Jachin also represent the two hemispheres of the brain. Boaz represents the right brain and is associated with the abstract, creative, intuitive principle in man. Boaz is our higher spiritual nature. Jachin represents the left-brain hemisphere and is associated with logic and intellect, physicality and concreteness.

Boaz symbolises the animating source in creation, while Jachin symbolises both intellect and our physical, earthly aspects. Our lower nature is connected to Jachin but this does not make our lower, physical nature a bad thing. Think of Jachin as the darkness to Boaz's light; as the rain to Boaz's sunshine. Think of Boaz as the redeemer of Jachin, that is the light that clears the darkness; the sunshine that clears the rain. It is only when the two aspects of our nature do not have a redeemer that we become out of balance, which is what Jesus meant when he said man does not live on bread alone. In other words, man cannot live life solely dictated by left brain thinking. There must be a spiritual aspect that redeems the left brain thinking and brings balance.

When we enter a lodge, we walk between the two pillars Boaz and Jachin, along the centre line, without favouring the left or the right side. As such we symbolise equilibrium between the active and passive forces within us.

The two pillars are not the only Masonic symbol representing duality. The black and white checkered pavement known as the mosaic pavement or checkered floorboard is also a symbol of duality.

The book of Genesis tells us that as God created heaven and earth, he separated light from darkness, and thus duality began from the moment of creation. On the sixth day God created the duality of man, as Genesis 1:27 tells us: 'God created man in His own image, in the image of God He created him; male and female.'

Once again, this excerpt must be examined allegorically, not literally, to uncover the 'dark sayings' concealed beneath the words.

Genesis 1:27 does not refer to man's physical composition but rather his psychological make up. 'Male and female' represents man's passive and active nature; spiritual and material aspects; the duality of man.

The key to living in a world of dichotomies is to find balance therein – a balance between cause and consequence. This is the Socratic law of causality, so profound and powerful that it has been referred to as the 'Iron Law of Human Destiny'. It is Sir Isaac Newton's third law of motion which states: 'For every action, there is an equal and opposite reaction.'

Think of the dualities of life as a circuit flow. The dualities travel in opposite directions and create a flow that moves around your centre. Consider dualities as a battery with a negative and positive charge. When the two charges are balanced the result is an electrical charge which is a result of the harmony of the two opposing forces, or a harmony of dualities. The positive redeems the negative, and harmony is achieved.

The yin and yang symbol, known as the *Taijitu*, is another symbol of duality. Our levels of yin and yang vary continuously. When either yin or yang is out of balance, and too much of our crude nature is not redeemed/balanced out by our higher nature, we experience negative effects. The challenge is to balance yin and yang, to walk between Boaz and Jachin, to bring about harmony between the two hemispheres of your brain.

A cunning man

Masonic ritual tells us that GMHA was a 'cunning workman' and 'by whose cunning workmanship the Temple was so beautified and adorned.'

2 Chronicles 2:13 tells us that Hiram was skilled in seven areas.

1. Gold & Silver
2. Bronze & Iron
3. Stone & Wood
4. Purple & Blue
5. Fine linen & crimson
6. Marking and engraving
7. Accomplishing any plan given him

Whenever we see reference to the number 7, the symbolism is that of the seven chakras.

GMHA represents mastership of the seven chakras of the body.

As in Masonic ritual, the Bible also describes GMHA as a 'cunning' man. The word cunning is also used to describe a serpent, and the serpent is a symbol of rebirth and renewal. The 'cunning' serpent also symbolises the kundalini – the serpent energy/hidden power within each of us.

GMHA possessed tools that could pierce and shape stone. So here we have the symbolism of one who has mastered the seven chakras, who possesses the necessary tools to reshape stone (reshape his earthly/physical self) and is thereby able to enter into a spiritual rebirth/renewal.

Only a skilled craftsman (GMHA) with a controlled mind has the power to raise the internal kundalini energy upwards through the seven chakras on its way to the pineal gland. The energy winds up the spine in a snake-like motion and is often referred to as the coiled serpent.

Raising the kundalini energy enables the skilled craftsman to unify the physical with the mental; the horizontal (level/physical) with the perpendicular (plumb rule/spiritual). The joining of the horizontal and the perpendicular produces the square.

2 Chronicles describes GMHA as a cunning man who worked in gold and silver. Gold is symbolic of the Sun, representative of the male aspect of our nature. Silver is symbolic of the moon, representative of the female aspect of our nature. GMHA is in perfect harmony with the male and female aspects of his duality. He is the symbolic centre line between the two pillars; a higher consciousness completely unpolarised.

GMHA is what American clairvoyant, 'The Sleeping Prophet' Edgar Cayce, would have described as a superconscious mind. Cayce revealed that humans have three different dimensions of awareness:

- The CONSCIOUS Mind - personality
- The SUBCONSCIOUS Mind - soul
- The SUPERCONSCIOUS Mind – spirit

According to Cayce, an important goal in everyone's life is to awaken the superconscious mind to attain what he called at-one-ment with God.

The superconscious mind is known by many names in various religions and belief systems. They include:

- Buddha consciousness
- Christ consciousness
- The collective mind
- The collective Unconsciousness
- The Holy Spirit
- Brahman God
- The Clear White Light
- Higher Self

Cayce believed that Jesus became a Christ, that is the full manifestation of Christ consciousness – the perfect union of the human with the divine. The same could be said of GMHA. His ability to integrate his body-mind-spirit and achieve the union of the human with the divine is the secret (master's word) the three ruffians attempted to extract from him.

There is also another similarity between GMHA and Jesus.

Jesus was nailed to a cross. A cross is the intersection of a vertical and a horizontal. GMHA was struck with a 24-inch gauge and a square, which if laid over one another form a cross. The final death blow came from a heavy setting maul or hammer, such as that which would have been used to hammer the nails into Jesus' hands and feet at the crucifixion.

The heavy setting maul wielded by Jubelum connects to the forehead of GMHA. The forehead protects the brain. Therefore, the final death blow impacts GMHA's brain. This tells us that once the brain is destroyed, the body dies. One can live with a fake heart, one lung, or a new kidney, but one cannot live without a brain. To strike the forehead is to strike the Third Eye. Once this light is extinguished, so too is the physical body.

Do not take the story of GMHA's death and raising literally. These characters are archetypes in an ages-old allegory about overcoming one's lower nature and reconnecting with the Source, with Supreme Consciousness.

1 Kings 7:13 tells us that Hiram 'was filled with wisdom, understanding and skill, to work all works in brass'.

What here is the significance of brass? And why too were the pillars Boaz and Jachin made of brass?

Brass is an alloy composed of copper and zinc. Zinc relates to the symbolic left brain and our physical lower nature. It is found in abundance in semen, which is representative of our lusts. Zinc is therefore symbolically attached to the pillar Jachin, being the symbolic left brain of our carnal desires.

Copper is a shiny metal and as such represents the symbolic right brain/illumination. Moses had a copper serpent. Copper is attached symbolically to the pillar Boaz, being the symbolic right brain of our spiritual nature/holistic thinking.

That GMHA was a skilled craftsman working in brass tells us that he mastered balance of the symbolic left brain and symbolic right brain, which is zinc and copper forming brass – perfect harmony.

Those Three Ruffians
GMHA is original consciousness, that is, the pure, higher consciousness of which we all once were.

The violence of the ruffians represents the fall of higher consciousness into the realm of the physical; into lower consciousness. You may have heard this descent of higher consciousness into physical matter referred to as The Fall of Man.

Note that the three ruffians only assault GMHA *after* he has exited the

Sanctum Sanctorum, or Holy of Holies, where he conducts his daily prayers (meditation).

While in the Sanctum Sanctorum – the place where God is said to reside – GMHA is safe from the violence of the ruffians and the outside world. He is pure, higher conciousness, unaffected and unblemished by the physical world. It is in the Sanctum Sanctorum – the pineal gland/ Peniel/place where Jacob saw God face to face – that GMHA experiences connection to the Source/God/Supreme Consciousness. He goes inside himself and in the darkness of the Sanctum Sanctorum, he sees the Light.

We read on the website originalteaching.com: 'When you have focused your attention correctly you will experience total blackness and total silence. There will be no images, lights, sights, sounds or thoughts of any kind. You will have entered the Nothingness, a state where soul doesn't exist, you will have entered the Holy of Holies wherein the mind-Father connection is made.'

As soon as GMHA leaves the protection/safety of the Sanctum Sanctorum he exposes himself to the dangers of the physical world/lower nature. He tries to escape the three ruffians via three gates of the temple – the South, West and East gates – but is blocked at every attempt. The three gates represent our base faculties, by none of which GMHA could be saved.

The workmen of the temple are alerted to GMHA's absence because there are no new designs on the trestle board. When our lower nature, represented by the three ruffians, kills our spiritual consciousness, represented by GMHA, consciousness is prevented from drawing any more designs.

The three ruffians continue an ancient esoteric symbol of the three traitors to our higher consciousness as seen in stories including:
• The three traitors to Jesus – Judas, Pilate and Caiphas
• The three Egyptian demons who killed Osiris
• The three traitors of the Old Testament – leaders of a revolt against Moses and Aaron

The higher consciousness, which is still inside us (our divine spark), is buried in the shallow grave of the body, just as GMHA was buried in a shallow grave.

Why shallow? Because the depths of the body are not deep. The shallow grave tells us that our higher consciousness buried there is accessible and can be raised if you know the means by which to do so.

A sprig of acacia is placed at the head of the shallow grave to remind us that the eternal, divine part of us – our higher consciousness – is still alive and can never die.

Acacia comes from the Greek word, *Akakia,* meaning innocence/free from corruption. This is the divine spark in each of us, our highest consciousness, free from corruption and blemishes. Interestingly, when written in Greek the named Hiram means 'unblemished'.

Through the grip of the Lion's Paw, using the strength of the Lion (love) of the Tribe of Judah (the Nation of Light) that camps at the East (right brain), GMHA (higher consciousness) is raised from his shallow grave (lower consciousness/ego), and the higher self is separated from the lower physical self.

The three ruffians – JubelA, JubelO and JubelUM – represent the earthly/physical, or the psychological 'I', the ego, the 'me, myself,'. Their names are the feminine suffix (A), male suffix (O) and neutral suffix (UM) derived from Jabal, the founder of Geometry.

Geometry is a science that measures the Earth (physical), and the 5th of the Seven Liberal Arts and Sciences. The number 5 relates to the five senses of the human body. We therefore know that the symbolism of the ruffians is all physical.

Jubela, Jubelo and Jubelum certainly do possess the three necessary components needed for raising consciousness – as do we all – but they do not have the knowledge or ability to combine these three components.

GMHA represents the integration of the three components needed to raise consciousness: the mind/soul, body and spirit.

Writes Samael Aun Weor: 'Perfect mental equilibrium is of vital importance for those who want spiritual progress. Almost all the aspirants of esotericism easily lose their mental equilibrium and usually fall into the most absurd things. Whosoever yearns for direct knowledge must ensure that their minds are in perfect equilibrium.'

The three ruffians represent how our higher consciousness becomes trapped in the physical realm. They are the three dimensions of our physical world:

1. Jubela – assaults with a 24-inch gauge. 24 hours of the day. Represents TIME
2. Jubelo – assaults with a square. A square measures space. Represents SPACE
3. Jubelum – assaults with a heavy setting maul. The killing blow. Represents DEATH.

They also represent our physical nature, intellectual nature and emotional nature, and correspond to the three gates, West, East and South, by which GMHA tries to make his escape. There is no escape, however, from these lower three realms of creation while in physical existence. You cannot escape thinking, feeling and action. There is no escape from physical death, and neither of these gates will release you from the ego's shackles to a state of higher consciousness.

The physical nature/intellectual nature/emotional nature – the three ruffians – must be killed off, but until then these three will kill you spiritually.

The dramatisation of the death and raising of the spiritual body of GMHA serves as a roadmap describing the proper function and potential of the human being.

The end goal here is the realisation of a state of being – a consciousness – higher than that which we currently exhibit. Our higher consciousness is in a state of potential which we presently contain.

So long as lower thoughts (the three ruffians demanding the word of a Master Mason) drive your life, you will fail to obtain higher consciousness. Through meditation, the lower thoughts are killed off (King Solomon put the three ruffians to death) so that higher consciousness can emerge. (Note: it was only after the execution of the three ruffians that King Solomon raised the spiritual body of GMHA, and not before).

The aim of the three ruffians (lower nature) is clear: attain higher consciousness. They fail to attain this state through their assault of GMHA, and so after burying the body in a shallow grave, they set off for the sea port of Joppa which, as mentioned earlier, symbolises a gateway to higher consciousness. There they ask a seafaring man to provide them passage to Ethiopia (also signifying higher consciousness – or the ruffians' perception of higher consciousness) but are refused.

There is no quick and easy way to gain higher consciousness. Such attainment cannot be accomplished through symbolic left brain thinking, which is what the ruffians are attempting to do.

The ruffians have tried to burst suddenly into bloom and obtain the master's word – the key to higher consciousness – without building their virtues slowly and carefully.

When we try to be something we are not, we often land in hot water.

The only method to self-improvement and transcending your lower nature is through gradual development and growth, as symbolised in Freemasonry by the Winding Staircase. Via the Winding Staircase, you gradually transmute your entire nature into the thing you desire to be. To grow gradually in a balanced manner is the secret to success. The three ruffians did not adhere to this process.

The ruffians and GMHA are comparable symbolically to Pharaoh and Moses. They are archetypes that portray opposing aspects of the human mind/soul in its relationship to Spirit.[28]

Pharaoh (the ruffians) is the limited ego-mind/soul. It sees itself as separate from the Universal Mind.

Moses (GMHA) represents the higher consciousness that is in direct connection with the Universal Mind, or man spirit in connection with God spirit.

Both Pharaoh and Moses are present in us all. The ruffians' stubbornness, their failure to obtain the master's word, and their failure to gain passage to Ethiopia, are our failures. We fail when we give in to our ruffian-like ego, when we accept it and accept its goals as our own.

The ruffians think they are separate from God, and everyone else. They live in the temporal, sensual world. Like GMHA and Moses, we must make the decision to rid ourselves of ego and follow the guidance of the Spirit.

It should also be noted that in the Masonic allegory of GMHA's death, fifteen Fellowcrafts were originally involved in the plot to kill the Grand Master. Twelve Fellowcrafts decided not to follow through with the evil plan, and only three – Jubela, Jubelo and Jubelum – remained to perform the deadly deed.

The twelve Fellowcrafts who recanted represent the 12 cranial nerves of the human brain.

The twelve cranial nerves are: Olfactory, Optic, Oculomotor, Trochlear, Trigeminal, Abducens, Facial, Auditory, Glosso-pharyngeal, Pneumogastric (or Vagus), Spinal accessory, and Hypoglossal. All of these are controlled by the brain.

The three Fellowcrafts who followed through with their deadly deed symbolise three things that cannot be controlled by the brain: Time, Space and Death.

We change the course of our life with mental power. Freemasonry teaches you how to subdue your passions and raise your mind from the animalistic level (the ruffians) to the higher plane (GMHA).

Be ye transformed by the renewing of your mind!

Breaking it down

Here is a basic breakdown of the events and symbolism surrounding GMHA's death and raising.

- GMHA symbolises higher consciousness.
- The three ruffians represent the three inescapable dimensions of our physical world: TIME, SPACE, DEATH; They kill GMHA, symbolically bringing higher consciousness down to the physical/animal/lower plane.
- GMHA (higher consciousness) is placed in a shallow grave (the human subconscious, just beneath the surface of our thoughts)
- A sprig of acacia is placed at the head of the grave, symbolising that even though the physical body is dead, there is an immortal part of man (higher consciousness) that can never die.
- King Solomon clears his mind (meditates) to quiet the clutter of the left brain and uses the strength of the Lion (love) of the Tribe of Judah (right brain/light) to raise GMHA from the grave (separate the higher consciousness from the lower self).

What? The builder!

Picture of a pluripotent stem cell from Austrailian Academy of Science.

Masonic Point within a Circle between two perpendicular parallel lines. It is a stem cell situated within a bone (bone marrow).

Upon being raised, the newly made Master Mason hears the word 'Mahabone' whispered in his ear. We are told that Mahabone means, 'What? The builder!' and was the first word uttered at GMHA's gravesite upon discovery of his lifeless body.

This word became the 'substitute' for the real word of a Master Mason which was lost with GMHA's untimely passing.

Mahabone is more than a word meaning 'What? The Builder!'. Like everything else in Freemasonry, it has a deeper meaning than what we are told in the ritual.

In keeping with the hidden brain science of Freemasonry uncovered in this book, we relate the word Mahabone back to the body, brain and nervous system. As such its real meaning is 'Marrow of the Bone' or, simply, 'Bone Marrow'.

In researching the KJV Old Testament Hebrew Lexicon, one of the translations for the word 'Machah' is 'full of marrow'.[29] 'Machah Bone' becomes Mahabone and translates as 'Marrow of the Bone' or 'Bone Marrow'.

Bone marrow is a semi-solid, spongy tissue found in portions of our bones. It is the primary site of new blood cell production or hematopoiesis. About 4% of our total body mass is bone marrow which produces approximately 200 billion blood cells per day.

Most blood cells in the body develop from cells in the bone marrow. The two types of bone marrow are red bone marrow, known as myeloid tissue, and yellow bone marrow, or fatty tissue.

Great amounts of oxygen are required for brain activity, and the brain receives its share of oxygen before all other organs of the body. The next part of the body to utilise available oxygen is bone marrow.

The replenishing of oxygen needed to keep our brain and bone marrow active is done through breathing. This is the reason why of all the words in Freemasonry, only Mahabone is to be delivered strictly in low breath (a whisper).

The oxygen we breathe in is carried through our circulatory system via the haemoglobin contained in our red blood cells. These red blood cells are produced in the bone marrow. The more oxygen the bone marrow receives, the more red blood cells are produced.

White blood cells, which are the base of our immune system, are also produced in the bone marrow.

When we reduce excessive tension and chatter in our brains (quiet the left brain), and maintain a calm presence in total mindfulness (right brain/'my mind is now clear') more blood cells carry to our bone marrow. As a result, the bone marrow produces even greater amounts of blood cells which increases oxygen to feed the brain and other body parts.[30]

Let's talk about stem cells, to which I believe the word Mahabone (bone marrow) is specifically directed.

Bone marrow contains stem cells. Stem cells are specifically the 'builder' referred to in Mahabone's translation as 'What? The Builder!'

Stem cells are best described as magical building blocks in the body. Adult stem cells travel to damaged tissues in our body and repair them by becoming those tissues. Consider stem cells a magic brick that can make the foundation as well as the wall, the foot path, the garage, the porch, and all other areas of a house.

Adult stem cells in your bone marrow constitute your body's natural healing system. When you're injured, stem cells are released from the bone marrow to the injury. They migrate to the damaged organ and become healthy cells of that organ. Amazingly, adult stem cells placed on a liver, muscle tissue or brain will quickly become that liver, muscle tissue or brain.

Stem cells are the building blocks of life. Their task is to build, regenerate and repair.

They are the builders of the physical Temple and are referred to as 'Master Cells'!

According to a report on the US Department of Health & Human Services website, a new study suggests that some cells from bone marrow can enter the human brain and generate new neurons and other types of brain cells.

If researchers can find a way to control these cells and direct them to damaged areas of the brain, this finding may lead to new treatments for stroke, Parkinson's disease, and other neurological disorders.

'This study shows that some kind of cell in bone marrow, most likely a stem cell, has the capacity to enter the brain and form neurons,' says Èva Mezey, MD, Ph.D., from HHS' National Institute of Neurological Disorders and Stroke (NINDS), who led the study.

Harvesting the correct type of stem cells, which would involve finding a way to create stem cells that are as powerful as embryonic stem cells from adult stem cells, could lead to the healing of all injuries, the replacement of worn-out organs, and the eradication of disease.

What does all this have to do with the word Mahabone uttered at the gravesite of GMHA?

The word Mahabone is the ritual writers' way of telling us that stem cells (produced in bone marrow) is the ultimate solution to maintaining a healthy brain for as long as possible. The ritual consistently tells us how to tap into the brain's full potential. We learn how to use our brain in meditation, how to differentiate the right and left hemispheres of our brain, and as we now see, it also teaches us how to physically sustain a healthy brain.

Mahabone – What? The Builder! – is a direct reference to bone marrow and stem cells as the BUILDER of the human body, capable of building, repairing and regenerating the brain.

'The Builder!' is not intended as an exclamation about the discovery of GMHA's lifeless body, but of the discovery of stem cells as the real Grand Master, Architect and Builder of the brain (temple) and the rest of your body.

We not only have the word Mahabone as proof of this but a symbol, too.

The familiar Masonic symbol of a Point Within a Circle bound by two perpendicular parallel lines is the same as the scientific illustration of a stem cell.

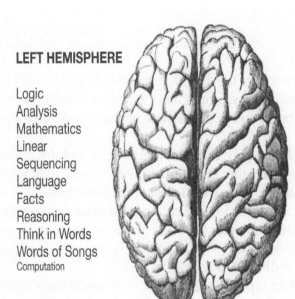

LEFT HEMISPHERE

Logic
Analysis
Mathematics
Linear
Sequencing
Language
Facts
Reasoning
Think in Words
Words of Songs
Computation

RIGHT HEMISPHERE

Creativity
Imagination
Holistic Thinking
Arts
Intuition
Non-Verbal
Tunes of Songs
Daydreaming
Visualisation

More than Meets the Eye

Is there any doubt that at its depths Freemasonry is a neurological handbook?

It is evident that there is more to Freemasonry than meets the eye. There are levels upon levels of Masonic lessons to be learned for those willing to peel away the layers of the onion.

At surface level Freemasonry is a 'beautiful system of morality, veiled in allegory and illustrated by symbols.' But as we have seen, Freemasonry is more than this much-used description.

You are now seeing, no doubt for the first time, the hidden Masonic symbolism of the human brain. You are seeing proof that the true purpose of Freemasonry is to re-energise the body, the glands, the nerve centres, the brain, etc., so as to reactivate the dormant pineal gland, open the inner spiritual eye, and ignite the divine spark.

It is all about the brain and the mind. The human brain is Solomon's Temple!

The story of GMHA and the three ruffians is not meant to be taken literally. It never actually happened!

Freemasonry's characters, lessons, lectures, and symbols are universal teachings to the potentialities of human consciousness. When read gnostically, employing the intuition and imagination of the symbolic right brain hemisphere, Freemasonry's teachings become a metaphysical treatise and a neurological pathway aimed at one thing only: self-improvement.

W.L. Wilmshurst described it best in the first chapter of *The Meaning of Masonry,* when he wrote:

It is well to emphasise, then, at the outset, that Masonry is a sacramental system possessing, like all sacraments, an outward and visible side consisting of its ceremonial, its doctrine and its symbols which we can see and hear, and an inward, intellectual and spiritual side, which is concealed behind the ceremonial, the doctrine and the symbols, and which is available only to the Mason who has learned to use his spiritual imagination and who can appreciate the reality that lies behind the veil of outward symbol. Anyone, of course, can understand the simpler meaning of our symbols, especially with the help of the explanatory lectures; but he may still miss the meaning of the scheme as a vital whole. It is absurd to think that a vast organisation like Masonry was ordained merely to teach grown men of the world the symbolical meaning of a few simple builders' tools, or to impress upon us such elementary virtues as temperance and justice – the children in every village school are taught such things.

−9−
A Neuroscientific Approach

Freemasonry is many things to many people depending on which direction you approach the Craft. A neuroscientific approach, as detailed in this book, leads to a world of immense benefits for the brain.

Research suggests that any activity involving thinking and learning is beneficial for brain health and protecting against dementia. More complex and challenging mental activities provide greater benefits to the brain. The more frequently your brain is challenged with complex activity, the lower your risk of dementia.

The key to healthy brain exercise is challenging the brain through activities that provide enjoyment, not stress. Attempting to undertake mental activities you consider boring may lead to stress and frustration, which is unhealthy for the brain.

Irish researchers found that through extended exercises in rote learning, learners recall more information overall. Rote learning benefits the hippocampal formation, a key structure in the brain for episodic and spatial memory in humans. In their group of participants aged 55-70, these researchers noted that repeated activation of memory structures promotes neuronal plasticity in the ageing brain.

Memory-forming can become a healthy lifelong habit. Researchers from the National Institute on Health and Ageing found that adults who went through short bursts of memory training were better able to maintain higher cognitive functioning and everyday skills, even five years after going through the training. Practicing memorisation allowed the elderly adults to delay typical cognitive decline by seven to 14 years.

High operating individuals

My lodge in Las Vegas, Nevada, is an extraordinary place. The Brethren who I presided over as Worshipful Master in 2016 are among the most inspirational men I have met, particularly the older Brethren. They include Pearl Harbor survivor, Edward Hall, 33rd degree Mason, Past Master, and at the age of 94 one of the most mentally acute men I know.

From my seat in the East I would gaze in wonderment at Ed every week, as he mouthed the words of the ritual from the sidelines and dressed as he was in a three-piece suit, his blue/grey eyes sparkling beneath a head of wavy silver hair. At 94, Ed still knew every word of every degree, cut clean, crisp signs, and took all the necessary steps. When at refreshment, he would sit at a table with other nonagenarians, octogenarians, and septuagenarians and engage in long discussions, not about sickness, pensions or war stories, but about such subjects as quantum physics, spirituality, history and philosophy.

Ed was not the only Brother in his eighties and nineties to present a razor-sharp brain and a healthy body. We also had an 80-something former special forces policeman; an 80-something Arc Light One survivor who was one of America's most decorated fighter pilots; an 80-something former accountant who had presided as Worshipful Master of a lodge in 1961; and a 90-something organist whose fingers still moved across the keys so fast as to be a blur. Each of these men were among the highest vibrational beings I have ever met, almost as if they were tuned to a different frequency than the rest of us.

Amazed by the physical and mental sprightliness of these Brothers, I made an effort to ask each and every one what was the secret to not only their longevity, but to the quality of life they each possessed. Their answers varied, of course, including such insights as 'a glass of wine a day,' 'organic foods,' 'plenty of sunshine' and the like, but the one answer common to each was, simply, 'Freemasonry.'

'Freemasonry saved me,' said Don Harten, who as a B-52 pilot survived a mid-air crash from what was intended to be the first B-52 raid on North Vietnam (Arc Light One Mission). Don's miraculous story of survival includes the mid-air crash of two B-52s, his rescue by a seaplane that crashed on takeoff, and finally his successful rescue by a freighter. 'I was a mess. The VA said I had the worst case of PTSD they had ever seen. The only thing that brought me back from the brink, the thing that saved my life, was Freemasonry.'

As passionate now as when he joined the Craft years ago, Don decided to join the officers' line as a Junior Steward in my lodge despite his age.

Don, Ed and the other Brothers I spoke to said that Freemasonry played a major role in their quality of life, but none of them could pinpoint in specific terms just how Freemasonry had contributed to their mental acuity. But there had to be a specific answer to exactly how Freemasonry had helped strengthen the brain of these older Brothers, and as a relatively young Mason myself, I went in search of an answer.

Brain changing

In my research I came across an article on the website www.faithandhealthconnection.org in which Rita Hancock, MD, a graduate of Cornell University interviewed Dr Andrew Newberg on his research about God and the brain, and his book, *How God Changes Your Brain.*[31] Reading the interview, I came across the specific answer for which I was searching.

Dr Rita asked Dr Newberg if thoughts literally change your brain, to which he answered: 'Yes, it is really a two-way street. Your brain changes your thoughts and your thoughts change your brain. The more you focus on a particular belief or belief system, the stronger those connections become. If you focus on God being loving and compassionate, you increase the amount of love and compassion in your brain, and your outward behaviours. If you focus on God being vengeful and hateful, you increase the amount of hate and anger in your brain, and your outward behaviours. As the saying goes, neurons that fire together wire together, and this is true no matter what our beliefs are. The more we focus on something, the more it becomes a part of how our brain functions.'

The octogenarians and nonagenarians in my lodge have been members of the Craft for 50 and 60 years – that's a lot of firing and wiring, and decades of focus on a constant message of faith, charity, hope; the tenets of Brotherly Love, Relief and Truth; the Cardinal Virtues of Temperance, Fortitude, Prudence and Justice; and long dedication to a particular method of self-improvement and brain science. As no lodge is ever opened without first giving thanks to Deity, these men had also been practising regular thanks to a higher power/Supreme Consciousness/the Universal Mind. It came as no surprise that further research led me to discover that practising gratitude, which Freemasons do in every lodge session, affects the brain in a number of positive ways, including:

- flooding the brain with positive chemicals
- calming anxiety
- lessening the effects of depression
- activating the limbic system, specifically the hypothalamus, which makes our metabolism, hunger and other natural bodily functions work more smoothly.

- training the prefrontal cortex to retain positive information over negative aspects of life.

Getting back to Dr Rita's interview with Dr Newberg, she next asked him about the health benefits of meditation and prayer, both of which are an important part of most religious systems and, of course, are an important part of the neuroscience of Freemasonry.

'There is certainly a fair amount of overlap between meditation and certain types of prayer,' answered Dr Newberg. 'We studied nuns doing centering prayer which, as you know, is a more contemplative practice. These types of prayer practices certainly should affect the brain in similar ways as other types of meditative/contemplative practices. For example, in centering prayer, we saw increased activity in the frontal lobes and decreased activity in the parietal lobes (this is believed to be associated with the sense of self and decreased activity is associated with losing that sense of self and feeling connected to the universe or God). Other types of Christian practices affect the brain slightly differently. We performed a study on the rosary and showed that it reduced anxiety significantly. The combination of its meaning and the ritualised elements, probably suppress the activity in the amygdala and reduce anxiety and fear in people. Other practices such as conversational prayer activate social areas of the brain and, when combined with feelings of love and compassion, likely reduce stress and anxiety, as well as spill over to enhancing a person's social interactions.'

Again, I found all this information highly relatable to Freemasonry and the practice of ritual performed in the lodge.

Next, Dr Rita asked: 'Would you say that attending a positive and healthy church might be good for the PHYSICAL body? Does research support that?'

Talking to my elderly Brothers, I too wondered if attending a positive and healthy lodge for so many years, with the performance of signs, steps and floor work, might be good for the physical body.

Answered Dr Newberg:

Absolutely, it can be good. The more you activate the positive emotions, derive meaning and optimism, access social support, and engage the brain in music, movement, and contemplation, the better it is for your whole body and brain. Lower levels of stress and anxiety lower the amount of the stress hormone cortisol. Since cortisol suppresses the immune system, lower levels help improve the immune system's function, and reduce blood pressure and heart rate, all of which can be beneficial. But as you alluded to, if the person is hearing about fear, anger, and guilt, they may not experience the same types of healthful benefits.

The candidate for Freemasonry is told at the very start of his journey to follow his conductor and 'fear no danger'. With the fear element deliberately removed, no sense of anger or guilt is ever directed towards the candidate.

Lodge rooms make use of music – indeed the Middle Chamber lecture goes into great detail about the importance of Music as one of the Seven Liberal Arts and Sciences – and constant movements such as the steps, penal signs and circumambulations of the lodge room, plus the social nature of Freemasonry, mean that Freemasons, according to Newberg's findings, would also reap the benefits of lower cortisol levels.

Dr Rita asked Newberg to talk about how fast your brain can change and what it takes to keep up those positive changes, to which he responded: 'It [the brain] is like a muscle, the more you work out, the bigger it becomes. In fact, brain scan studies have shown that the brains of long-term meditators literally are thicker than those who do not practice. We showed similar changes in terms of overall brain activity being higher in spiritual individuals who have done meditation or prayer for many years. But it is also true that you have to use it or lose it. If you stop focusing on a particular idea, the brain will lose that connection over time. That is good if the connection supports a destructive belief but can be bad if the connection supports a positive belief.'

Watching someone like Ed Hall mouth the ritual word for word week in, week out, is active proof of his brain training or, to use a Masonic phrase, the active polishing of his rough ashlar. The performance of ritual recited by heart, just as prayers are recited by heart, becomes a form of meditation, thus working out the brain with the consistency and vivaciousness of a bodybuilder exercising his muscles at the gym.

Memory work is a necessity of the Freemason, as all ritual is performed by memory, an open book not permitted in the lodge room. Dedication to memory work improves the limbic system of the brain, particularly the hippocampus and the amygdala. Memory work actually enlarges the hippocampus, which helps combat the negative effects of the amygdala, the part of the brain responsible for fear response. Memory work has been proven to ward off the onset of degenerative brain diseases such as Alzheimer's.

Masonic memory work and brain plasticity

Masonic memory work contributes to brain plasticity, also known as neuroplasticity, which is the brain's ability to change throughout an individual's life. In other words, brain plasticity can also be termed as the ability of the brain to modify its connections or reset (re-wire) itself.

This modification encompasses brain activity associated with a given function that can be transferred to a different location, the proportion of grey matter that is subject to change as well as the ability of synapses to strengthen or weaken over the course of an individual's life. Without this ability your brain would be unable to develop from childhood through to adulthood or recover from injury/trauma.

Brain plasticity offers contrary evidence to the previously held notion humans are born with a set number of brain cells that can never be replaced. However, studies now show that the brain is a continual work in progress.

How brain plasticity works

The brain is special and differs from a personal computer because it processes sensory and motor signals in parallel. What this implies is that the human brain has many neural pathways that can replicate another's function so that small errors in development or temporary loss of function through damage is rectified by redirecting signals along a different neural pathway. In summary, the brain is able to reorganise pathways, create new connections, and, in some cases, even create new neurons.

Importance of brain plasticity

Neuroplasticity is at the centre of control for pretty much all activity carried out by the different parts of the body. The brain is divided into areas that control certain functions in the human body. These control centres are predetermined by the work of genes.

For instance, consider that there is a region of the brain tasked with the responsibility of enabling the movement of the right hand. Any injuries to that part of the brain may impair the proper movement of the right hand. However, if another part of the brain that controls feelings/sensations in the right hand is untouched, the individual might be able to feel things with the hand in question but will be unable to move the arm.

In one sense, it might seem to be the case that one control centre in the brain may be unable to take on the role(s) of another damaged region of the brain. However, the human body, especially the brain, possesses remarkable healing properties. With proper care, it is possible that the damaged area of the brain can get better. Whether in lieu of or as a result, neuroplasticity shows the brain's dexterity in dealing with an adverse situation, with the creation of new neural connections.

Studies with test specimens showcase this phenomenon. Researchers induced a loss of the sense of touch in a type of nematode, which resulted in the organism developing a heightened sense of smell. As in the earlier case of the right hand, the loss of mobility can be said to be compensated with the individual feeling more aware of his/her sensory powers of touching/feeling.

Neuroplasticity also works alongside external stimulatory influences. Developing infants make use of sensory (visual, auditory, tactile, smell) and motor stimuli in creating new neural connections and functions. In the same vein, the more an individual has exposed sensory and motor stimulation, the better-enhanced neuroplasticity becomes, which ultimately helps in the recovery of the part of the brain that suffered damage or injury.

Brain plasticity and memory improvement

Neuroplasticity refers to the mechanism by which the brain decodes experience, learns new behavioural patterns and relearns forgotten/lost behaviour brought about by injury.

Research shows that neuroplasticity and ritualised learning are inter-dependent to very large extents. In other words, experience-dependent neuroplasticity suggests that the brain changes in response to what it experiences. A study to this effect was conducted with taxi drivers in the city of London, and the results proved outstanding. London taxi drivers undergo extensive training for two – four years, learning and committing street names to memory as well as the layout of streets within the city and the quickest cross-city routes.

Researchers then examined these drivers after the induction period and discovered that the grey matter component of their brains had grown appreciably over the period. This growth takes place in the posterior hippocampus, a region of the brain concerned with memory and retention.

Further investigation showed that the longer the taxi drivers navigated the streets of the city, the more the grey matter of the posterior hippocampus increased in volume. Scientists came to the conclusion that a correlation exists between the mental training/exercise an individual undergoes and the increase in his/her brain's capacity to manage increasing amounts of information and complex tasks.

The commitment to memory of Masonic ritual and large portions of text, such as the lectures associated with each degree, also increase the individual's brain capacity. Analysis of the brain of a skilled ritualist and Masonic lecturer would no doubt show greater grey matter growth in the posterior hippocampus.

Music and Freemasonry
Mental exercise is just as important as the physical variety when it comes to neuroplasticity, memory strengthening and the overall health/wellbeing of the brain.

An activity that is often recommended for keeping the processes of the brain at optimum levels is music. Musical practice promotes brain plasticity and improves various aspects of memory processing, retention, and retrieval.

The verbal rehearsal processes involved with singing or learning to play a musical instrument often precipitates improvements to verbal, working and long-term memory. With this in mind it is little wonder that the Fellowcraft degree places such emphasis on Music as one of the Seven Liberal Arts and Sciences.

Indeed, of all the seven, it is Music that receives the longest description in the Middle Chamber lecture, in which we are told: 'It is the medium which gives the natural world communication with the spiritual, and few are they who have not felt its power and acknowledged its expressions to be intelligible to the heart. It is a language of delightful sensations, far more eloquent than words.'

Use it or lose it
The term 'use it or lose it' aptly describes what happens when an individual stops assisting his/her brain's plasticity with supportive habits and systems.

People should engage in what researchers' term 'self-directed brain plasticity'. This involves taking steps to enhance brain plasticity, to keep it re-growing and re-energising. Attending every lodge meeting, undertaking to learn the ritual/lectures/working tools, etc., and participating in the offices of the lodge are all forms of self-directed brain plasticity.

Challenging yourself to memorise Masonic ritual is a means of keeping the brain healthy and creating new neural pathways to accommodate the receipt/processing of new information.

Oxytocin production

The lodge experience is communal. One or two people cannot open a lodge of Freemasons; a minimum of three Master Masons is required to open a lodge of Master Masons; five are required to open a lodge on the Fellowcraft degree; and seven is the minimum to open a lodge on the Entered Apprentice degree.

Being part of a communal atmosphere that promotes friendship, Brotherly Love, and good will towards one another, contributes towards the brain's production of oxytocin, otherwise known as the 'bonding chemical' and sometimes referred to as the 'friendship chemical' and the 'love hormone.' Oxytocin originates in the brain, where it's produced by the hypothalamus, and then transferred to the pituitary gland which releases it into the bloodstream. Levels of the hormone tend to be higher during socially bonding experiences, according to the American Psychological Association.[32]

Oxytocin promotes attachment, solidifies relationships, eases stress, crystallises emotional memories, and fosters generosity, which is especially important to the Freemason who extols Charity as one of the three principal rounds on Jacob's Ladder (the other two being Faith and Hope). In a 2007 study in the journal *Public Library of Science ONE*, participants inhaled oxytocin or a placebo through their noses, and were then given a decision on how to split money with a stranger. Those on oxytocin were 80 percent more generous, researchers said, and the hormone seemed to affect their sense of altruism as well.[33]

Ritual is key to success in Freemasonry's method of self-improvement, both in its memorisation and in the internalisation of its lessons.

The aim of a participant in any ritual is to achieve a psychological state that is different from the state the participant began in. The performance of the ritual is known as ceremony. The words themselves, as spoken during the ceremony, are known as ritual. It is within the wording and subtext of the ritual that the Freemason finds the real lessons of the Craft. How much the Mason wishes to learn, how much he wishes to probe and analyse and engross himself in the depths of Masonic literature and symbolism, to see how deep the teachings run, is a pursuit for he and he only. One gets out of Freemasonry whatever one chooses to put into it.

Author Rudyard Kipling, himself a passionate Freemason who was initiated in the Lodge of Hope and Perseverance, No. 782, India, wrote of the importance of ritual: 'To know the ritual is not to know all – it is the inside meaning, not the words, that count – learn the words but get the Ritual into your spirit.'

Elevate consciousness

The end aim of Freemasonry is to elevate consciousness. To elevate consciousness, we must first affect consciousness, which is done through activating the intuition. In his essay entitled *The Magic of Masonic Ritual*, Brother Akram R. Elias writes[34]: 'We know that rituals, through symbolism, make lasting impressions upon a man's consciousness... consciousness plays a paramount role in influencing physical behaviour, and if one were to alter his own consciousness, he could ultimately alter his behaviour.'

Brother Elias writes further that:

A man through ritual can affect his consciousness by letting symbols affect his senses and activate his intuition; and an altered state of consciousness ultimately expresses itself in tangible actions. In Freemasonry, that is exactly the purpose of ritual. As Masons we believe that Freemasonry takes good men and makes them better. Indeed, it is through its richly moral rituals that Freemasonry makes such a deep and lasting impact on the individual brother. By altering one's own level of consciousness, a good man can make himself better through a gradual process of internal change. This is true alchemy and therefore the most important aspect of Masonic ritual.

Meditation is another method of positively affecting one's consciousness. Whilst many perceive meditation as sitting cross-legged under a waterfall with eyes closed, I believe there are various forms of meditation that positively affect the brain. Freemasonry's emphasis on secrecy is actually an emphasis on silence, which is one of the key aspect is the spring of acacia in Masonic rituals to successful meditation. From the moment the candidate for Freemasonry first enters the lodge room, he is eschewed to maintain the secrets of the Craft. But what secrets does the Entered Apprentice actually know? None! Therefore, it is really silence that he is promising to observe.

Real alchemy

Dedicated Freemasons, such as Brother Ed Hall, are true alchemists who transmute mundane thoughts into the gold of altered consciousness. Through the neuroscientific lessons contained in Masonic ritual, they undertake weekly workouts of their brain producing tangible results evident to all, like myself, who have had the thrill of witnessing the higher vibrational frequency on which these men operate. A Freemason like Ed Hall operates with an extremely high level of intelligence quotient (IQ), emotional quotient (EQ) and spiritual quotient (SQ), being the ability to perceive truth in oneself and to see the truth of others, and be better able to find enjoyment, beauty and purpose in life.[35]

– 10 –
An inside job

The Charge at Passing in the Fellowcraft degree ritual states: 'The internal, not the external qualifications of a man are what Masonry regards.'

These are among the most important words in the entirety of Masonic ritual and should be firmly imprinted on your mind both as a means to live your life and a means with which to view the world.

From a macrocosmic viewpoint, this part of the Charge tells us, simply, to never judge a book by its cover, that is, never make assumptions about anyone on their appearance alone. One should not form an opinion on someone or something based purely on what is seen on the surface, because after taking a deeper look, the person or thing may be very different from what was expected.

The phrase to 'never judge a book by its cover' dates back to at least the mid-19th century as seen in the newspaper *Piqua Democrat*, June 1867: 'Don't judge a book by its cover, see a man by his cloth, as there is often a good deal of solid worth and superior skill underneath a jacket and pants.'

As we have seen with the wording of the Charge at Passing, the concept of not judging a man by his external appearance was part of Masonic teaching long before what was written in *Piqua Democrat*.

It is difficult to change the superficiality of our nature. Sight is our most powerful physical sense – the visual area occupies 30 percent of our cortex at the back of our brain. We're often attracted to the shiniest, flashiest and most beautiful objects, perceiving them to be inherently 'better' than those less shiny.

Our most powerful sense
How powerful is your vision?

The retina is a thin layer of tissues that lines the inside of the eye at the rear, located near the optic nerve. The retina's job is to receive light focused by the lens, convert this light into neural signals, and relay those signals to the brain for visual recognition.

An outgrowth of the brain, the retina contains 150 million light-sensitive rods and cone cells. In the actual brain, there are hundreds of millions of neurons devoted to visual processing which take up almost a third of the brain. Compare this to the 8 percent of the brain dedicated to touch and 3 percent for sound; the millions of fibres comprising the two optic nerves compared to only 30,000 fibres in each auditory nerve, and you get an idea as to the power of your sense of sight.

Signals from the retinas are conveyed via the optic nerves to two structures, called the lateral geniculate bodies, in the thalamus region of the brain. The thalamus, as explained earlier, is a massive relay station for processing sensory messages from all parts of the body.

The signals then proceed to the V1, or primary visual cortex at the back of the brain. They then proceed to a second processing area, V2, before moving onto higher centres responsible for such jobs as detecting detail, depth, movement, shapes, colour, and facial recognition.

We all do it

Humans are visual creatures. We can't help it! Thirty percent of our cortex is dedicated to vision.

Marketing companies make billions developing strategies to engage our sense of vision. Bright wrappings, bows, ribbons, and eye-catching logos are all designed to create an attraction and build expectation.

Dr Martin Luther King Jr. once said: 'Our problem today is that we have allowed the internal to become lost in the external. We have allowed the means by which we live to outdistance the ends for which we live.'

He was right.

King believed we lived in two realms: the internal and the external. The internal realm is the realm of art, literature, rituals, morals, and poetry. It is the cultural expression. The external realm comprises the techniques, mechanisms, instruments and devices by which we live.

The internal realm develops our purpose in life. Only the internal realm gives us the power to 'subdue our passions', that is, to tame the ego and develop our purpose in life. This, of course, is the duty of every Freemason, as detailed at the opening of the lodge during this exchange between the Worshipful Master and the Senior Warden:

WM: What came you here to do?

SW: To learn to subdue my passions and improve myself in Masonry.

Unless one can master the internal realm, that is subdue the passions – control the ego – one cannot improve oneself in Masonry, which as detailed earlier is the progressive science of self-improvement, amongst other things.

The external realm is the realm that the eye perceives. It is our clothes, our car, our house, our physical appearance, our bank account – the means by which we live in the physical world, and the means by which the world perceives us.

Most of us are dominated by our external realm, paying little to no attention to the interior realm. We live in a reality defined by King whereby our technical power has control over our cultural power, that is, our external is given greater strength than our internal, leading to a weakening of our critical thinking, creativity and analysis, and a lessening of our intuitive and spiritual aspects.

Remember, the wrapper on something is not as important as the contents inside. Without proper refrigeration and maintenance, the contents of a beautiful looking carton of milk will soon spoil and turn sour.

The 'Royal Art'

Freemasonry is sometimes referred to as the 'Royal Art'.

Why is this? What qualifies Freemasonry as 'art'?

'The aim of art,' said Aristotle, 'is to represent not the outward appearance of things, but their inward significance.'

This is the purpose of Freemasonry, which may be described as The Royal Art of Interpretation of Symbol and Allegory. Why royal? Because it is the glory of God to conceal a thing, and the glory of KINGS to discover it.

Through Masonic ritual, words and symbols, we strengthen our internal realm and express our own inward significance. As such we are taught to not give too much value to the surface, lest we miss the value beneath.

The images – the symbols, the signs, the steps – are outward, but the reflection is inward. We only rise above ourselves by going inward and returning to the Source, leaving the fixation on the body behind and going to the body's dynamic source – Supreme Consciousness.

Once again, you must grasp the internal and not the external aspects of Freemasonry's teachings. The literal interpretation of a symbol or allegory is never the correct one. Look deeper. Study the art to discover the hidden lesson.

Freemasons are told to study and follow the Holy Bible as our 'guiding light'. Within the pages of the Bible are lessons on the mind and spirit concealed in the 'dark sayings' or myths. The myths are metaphorical of spiritual potentiality in the human being, and the same powers that animate our life, animate the life of the world.

This is why Freemasonry places such a large emphasis on the Bible. Not because the lessons within the pages of the Old and New Testaments should be taken literally. The Bible tells us not to take its stories literally! It's all myth, all symbolic, all allegory! Jesus only spoke in parables, that is, he only spoke in allegory, never literally. The Bible is all mythology showing you how to overcome the lower mind, and raise your consciousness to the highest conscious state, to reconnect with Supreme Consciousness. That's why they're call Testaments. Testa (*testari*; Latin) – testify/bear witness to; Ment (*mente*; Latin) – mind. The Testaments are psychology books – they testify/bear witness to the workings of the mind!

Freemasonry knows this, which is why the Bible lecture in Masonic ritual tells us 'to study therein to learn the way to everlasting life'.

Again, 'everlasting life' does not mean everlasting physical life. It means everlasting cosmic life; everlasting consciousness. When Jesus ascended to heaven, he didn't actually, physically fly up through the clouds and zip off to an actual, physical place called heaven. To interpret the gospel as such is ludicrous! Jesus never ascended to heaven because there is no physical heaven anywhere in the universe.

The kingdom of heaven is inside you – the Bible tells us so!

2 Corinthians 6:16: 'You are the temple of the living God.'

2 Corinthians 3:16: 'Don't you know that you are the temple of God, and that the Spirit of God dwells in you?'

Luke 17:21: 'Neither shall they say, Lo here! or, lo there! for, behold, the kingdom of God is within you.'

How many more times do you need the Bible to flat out tell you that God is not external? The Bible is mythology. The temple is your brain, specifically the right hemisphere of your brain. God is internal! Supreme Consciousness is inside you, it is the sprig of acacia in Masonic ritual, that never, never, never dies.

Jesus went inward, not outward; he didn't ascend into outer space, he went into inner space – to the Source, Supreme Consciousness, the kingdom of heaven within.

The stone the builder rejected

The Mark Mason tells a story about a rejected stone heaved into the rubbish of the temple because it is neither oblong nor square and therefore (on appearance) considered useless to the temple builders.

Shortly after the stone is heaved into the rubbish, a calamity occurs on the building site. The workmen need a keystone to complete one of the main arches and finish the temple building, but no worker has been ordered to make such a keystone.

The Right Worshipful Master informs the workmen and overseers that he gave Grand Master Hiram Abiff strict orders to make such a keystone previous to his assassination and asks if such a stone has ever been brought forward for inspection. The Master Overseers inform the Right Worshipful Master that indeed such a stone was brought forward but owing to its impractical external appearance the stone was heaved into the rubbish.

The Right Worshipful Master orders that the stone be found as it is 'one of the most valuable stones in the whole building' and 'the Temple cannot be finished without it'. He declares: 'Let diligent search be made for it. It is the most important stone of the building. Richly rewarded shall he be who succeeds in recovering it'.

The workmen find the stone, which is then fitted to complete the arch and finish the building of the Temple.

There are many lessons to be learnt in the Mark degree, one of which is to keep an open mind and not reject things (particularly people) because they appear peculiar, different, or unknown.

Perception of the external prevents you discovering the true beauty of a person who may play an important role in your life. Do not judge harshly or condemn someone unjustly because they don't conform to your preconceived ideas, or because you don't understand them.

'You get nowhere looking at clothes and the colour of the skin to judge a man', said author Richard Puz. 'It won't tell you nothing about what's inside. That's where a fellow's mettle is, and that's what counts.'

It's all inside

Freemasonry is interior work that uses a degree system to progressively develop higher levels of consciousness, which leads to a greater understanding of one's self.

Once the interior work is undertaken, there is no turning back, just as you can't un-see something seen.

Writes W. Kirk MacNulty:

> When he has done it, when he has recognised himself to be an individual, like the Rough Ashlar cut from the mountain which will never be part of the bedrock again, the Entered Apprentice can never go back. To put it another way, when one has had an insight into his nature, when he has a glimpse of the fact

that he really is, inside, at the core of his being the 'Image of God', he can never unknow it.[36]

The symbols, wording and ritual of Freemasonry affects the candidate on a psychological level (internally), not on a physical level (externally). Belief in a Supreme Being is necessary because the object of elevating consciousness is to reconnect with Supreme Consciousness and become aware of the presence of Divinity within ourselves, which is the ignition of our divine spark.

The keystone in the Mark degree symbolises completion of the temple. As the temple symbolically represents you – your internal, spiritual self, that house not made with hands, eternal in the heavens – so the fitting of your keystone into the principal arch represents personal completion.

Completion (placement of the keystone) takes place when one reconnects with Supreme Consciousness, a large part of which lies in one's ability to harmonise with others. After all, as the ritual tells us, harmony is the support of all institutions, especially this of ours.

It is for this reason that we take an obligation not to admit women into our lodges. Says the Senior Warden in the ritual of opening the lodge: 'As the suns sets in the West at the close of day, so stands the Senior Warden in the West to assist the Worshipful Master in opening and closing the lodge, paying the craft their wages if any be due, that none may go away dissatisfied, harmony being the support of all institutions, especially this of ours.'

No women

Harmony is the force of Freemasonry, not money, power, membership, location or history. Anything that interferes with harmony would subsequently undermine the effectiveness of the foundation and strength of the institution.

You may consider yourself above having lewd thoughts about women, but no matter your age from the youngest Entered Apprentice to the octogenarian who wears his sixty-year lapel pin, it is man's nature to be attracted to the opposite gender.

Should this attraction occur during lodge meetings, as fleeting as it may be with a wandering eye or a titillating fantasy dashed from the imagination in a millisecond, it would serve to cause disharmony to that for which harmony is imperative.

Female presence in the lodge room is a distraction to the male mind. It is for harmony's sake that an obligation is taken to not permit women into Masonic lodges, and not make a woman a Mason.

Let me state, however, that nowhere in the ritual does it say a woman cannot become a Freemason. An obligation is taken to not initiate, pass or raise women as Freemasons, and to not allow the admission of a woman into a lodge room, but nowhere does it say a woman cannot become a Freemason.

As with all in Freemasonry, we must look beneath the surface for a deeper, esoteric meaning as to why we do not permit the admission of women into the lodge, remembering that the lodge is you! More specifically the lodge is your brain, your mind, your thoughts. As all is 'veiled in allegory and illustrated by symbols', there must be an allegorical and symbolic reason we 'forbid the admission of females into our assemblies'.

Let's return to the story of Samson and Delilah we visited earlier to understand the concealed teaching behind the obligation to not make a woman a Mason nor to allow the admission of women into the lodge.

When (allegorical) Samson allowed (allegorical) Delilah into his lodge room (his mind/his brain), it led to his spiritual demise. Delilah, the woman, represents our emotions. Once Samson gave into Delilah (emotions) and told her the secret of his (spiritual) strength, Delilah (emotions) had control over him and cut off his hair (his spiritual connection to God/higher mind/Supreme Consciousness). Having lost his hair (spiritual strength/higher mind) Samson was imprisoned by the Philistines (lower nature/ego).

The lesson here is to not be ruled by emotion, symbolised by woman, but to be ruled by the spirit/higher mind. Therefore, we do not admit women (emotions) into our lodge room (our brain/thought process) because allowing emotions to control our thoughts puts us at risk of spiritual demise. To break this obligation is to resort to our lower nature/ego/lusts at the expense of our higher nature, which is beyond the lusts and ego. Just as Samson was blinded by the Philistines after giving into his emotions (Delilah) so are we blinded by our lower nature if we give into our emotions.

Completing our mission
To complete our mission of elevating our consciousness so as to ignite our divine spark by reconnecting with Supreme Consciousness, we must learn

to see the internal qualifications of our fellow human beings and not be lost in the external, as Dr King taught.

Thus, when we are told that it is the internal not the external qualifications of a man that Freemasonry regards, we are being taught a major life lesson. It is for this reason that in most Masonic jurisdictions around the world, Freemasons dress in the same manner when attending lodge. As such there are no external characteristics that prove one Brother's wealth or social status from another. Dressed equally, all are the same from an external viewpoint. It is how we are dressed on the inside, the degree of Brotherly Love, Truth, and Relief we exhibit to our fellow man, and the Cardinal Virtues of Temperance, Fortitude, Prudence and Justice we embody that qualifies us as just and upright men and Masons.

– 11 –
The soul and the spirits

You do not have a soul, you are a soul. You are not a spirit, you have a spirit.

Throughout this book you will read many references to the three components of a human being: Mind, Body and Spirt.

This may confuse some of you who understand the three components of a person to be: Mind, Body, Soul. But as I will show you, the Mind and the Soul are one and the same, and despite what you think you know, the soul *is* corruptible and perishable. The spirit is not.

Soul and spirit are different
So, what is the difference between your soul and your spirit?

Your soul is life, it is consciousness, it is the mind. Your soul is immaterial, yet it is that part which animates the material.

You know that little voice in your head that never stops talking, never gets sick, is never late, never short of a word, and is with you from the moment you wake up until the moment you sleep? That's your soul. That's your mind. It is capable of good and bad.

Thinking, feeling, planning, organising, focusing or getting distracted – that's all the soul's doing. The soul is mind, will and emotions. The soul is pleasure or pain; positivity or discouragement. The soul forms words to communicate with others. The soul is the spring from which our personality flows. Anxiousness or peaceful rest are states of the soul.

When you hear of someone talking about the soul being untarnished and unblemished, such talk is not true. The soul is corruptible. It is not the beautiful, god-like part of you. It is not your connection to God/The Source/Universal Mind/Supreme Consciousness. That connection happens through the spirit.

The spirit is incorruptible. The spirit is the divine spark within. The spirit is the god-like part of you. It is your connection to Supreme Consciousness.

The soul possesses your good aspects and your bad aspects. The things you do in daily life, good or bad, are a result of the influence of the mind, and therefore the soul. As Luke tells us in his gospel: 'Human beings have a sinful nature, and our souls are tainted with sin.'

It is your spirit – let's call it your man spirit – that connects with the Holy Spirit/Supreme Consciousness. Says Romans 8:16: 'The Spirit Himself witnesses with our spirit – not the heart or the soul – that we are children of God.'

Your man spirit is the part of you that works together with the Holy Spirit. In other words, your higher consciousness is the part that works together with Supreme Consciousness.

The higher consciousness (man spirit) is the element in humanity that gives us the ability to have an intimate relationship with Supreme Consciousness (Holy Spirit).

In simple terms, the soul is the animate life, the seat of desires, affections, senses and appetites. The spirit is the part of us that connects to God.

A human is a three part being:
• Mind (soul)
• Body
• Spirit

This is made evident in 1 Thessalonians 5:23 where it is written: 'And the God of peace Himself sanctify you wholly, and may your spirit and soul and body be preserved complete...'

As we learn in Hebrews 4:12, the spirit and the soul are as separable as the body and the soul: 'For the word of God is living and effective and sharper than any double-edged sword, penetrating as far as the separation of soul and spirit, joints and marrow. It is able to judge the thoughts and intentions of the heart.'

If your soul and your spirit were one and the same, they would not be separable. But the above Bible verse clearly tells us that the soul and the spirit are two separate, immaterial aspects of a human being.

Distinct entities are separable. Think of it like water and sand. When mixed together, water and sand become sandy water. Although one thing (sandy water), it is still made up of two things (water and sand). If left undisturbed in a glass, the sand will settle at the bottom, thus separating from the water as they are two separate entities. Think of the soul and the spirit in the same manner.

The soul is a minefield

The soul is who you are in physical existence.

Your habits, your traits, your personality, your thought process, your choices to do right or wrong – that's all your soul's (mind's) doing.

The human soul is a mine field. All the thoughts you have in a day, approximately 70,000 of them, are the result of your soul (mind). It is the loud clutter of the mind that we attempt to quiet in meditation.

When Jesus told us to enter into our closet and pray, he did so because he understood how important it is to get away from the cacophony of the soul!

Your spirit has no part in the clutter of your thoughts, in your lusts, desires and ego. Your spirit is above all that is concerned with the flesh. In fact, the Bible tells us quite clearly that, 'the flesh lusts against the Spirit, and the Spirit against the flesh.' We are admonished to 'walk in the spirit' (symbolic right brain) so as to not fulfil the 'lust of the flesh' (symbolic left brain).

As two of the three components of a human being, the soul and spirit are intimately connected, but they are not the same.

The soul is the essence of your being. The spirit is that divine part of you that allows you to connect with the divine. It's the god-part of you.

When Jacob saw God face to face at the place he called Peniel, it was his elevated man spirit – his higher consciousness – that connected with God (Supreme Consciousness), not his soul.

By raising the master, we attempt to raise our spirit and attain our higher consciousness that places us in direct contact with Supreme Consciousness.

Polishing your soul and living through good thoughts and deeds – to which the Moral Science of Freemasonry is dedicated – chips away at the rough ashlar of your soul to transform it into a perfect ashlar. When this happens, you will begin responding to circumstances in line with your higher consciousness rather than your lower consciousness or physical senses.

All is energy

Quantum physics proves that physical atoms comprise vortices of energy that are constantly spinning and vibrating, each one radiating a unique energy signature.

We truly are beings of energy and vibration. Arjun Walia writes on the website collective-evolution.com:

If you observed the composition of an atom with a microscope you would see a small, invisible tornado-like vortex, with a number of infinitely small energy vortices called quarks and photons. These are what make up the structure of the atom. As you focused in closer and closer on the structure of the atom, you would see nothing, you would observe a physical void. The atom has no physical structure, we have no physical structure, physical things really don't have any physical structure! Atoms are made out of invisible energy, not tangible matter.[37]

Everything is energy vibrating at different frequencies, including our thoughts. 'If you want to find the secrets of the universe,' said Nicola Tesla, 'think in terms of energy, frequency and vibration'.

Albert Einstein said, 'Energy cannot be created or destroyed, it can only be changed from one form to another.' This is known as the Law of Conservation of Energy.

Interesting, isn't it?

Your thoughts resonate as vibrational energy. What you think dictates whether you vibrate at a higher or lower frequency. Negative thoughts produce negative energy, which vibrates at a lower frequency. Positive thoughts produce positive energy, which vibrates at a higher frequency.

Arjun Walia further writes: 'Studies have shown that positive emotions and operating from a place of peace within oneself can lead to a very different experience for the person emitting those emotions and for those around them.'

Manly P. Hall states: 'Vibrating at a very high rate of speed is the actual case of true spiritual illumination.'

Do different states of emotion, perception and feelings result in different electromagnetic frequencies?

'Yes!' writes Walia, 'this has been proven'.

Sabrina Reber on the website awakeningpeople.com:

When your vibration is low, your light particles are vibrating slowly and become condensed. Your energy literally feels heavy because you are not in alignment with your soul or divine self and are mostly operating from your lower self or ego. Distorted beliefs, fear, anger, resentment, blame, guilt, jealousy, judgment, shame, addiction, unforgiveness, conditional love, lack of self-worth, greed, separation consciousness and poor health keep you in very dense low vibrating energy. When you are a high vibrational being you recognise your divinity and the divinity within others. You are in alignment with your soul, which is nourished by spirit, you are vibrantly healthy and your life flows with ease and grace.

Freemasonry aims to manifest a new, higher vibrational you. The goal is to vibrate at the highest frequency possible so as to reconnect with Supreme Consciousness/God/The Source/Universal Mind. The greatest way to facilitate this reconnection is via the most powerful energy in the universe: love.

When death comes knocking

Man is a physical being with a spiritual component.[38] At death, the man spirit is separated from the soul and returns to the Holy Spirit who originally formed and placed it in the mind. In other words, upon death of the body, higher consciousness is separated from lower consciousness and returns to the Supreme Consciousness that originally formed and placed higher consciousness in the body.

Understand this: the body does not return to the source. The body is dead. It will never be reanimated. 'Flesh and blood,' so Paul tells us, 'cannot inherit the Kingdom of God.' Only higher consciousness can inherit connection to Supreme Consciousness.

All is energy. Consciousness is no exception. At the time of death, the body's spark of divine energy returns to the source energy. During physical life, elevation of this divine energy portion of the person allows greater connection with the source energy. Basically, heightening your consciousness above your lower nature allows you a connection with Supreme Consciousness.

The soul is not immortal. The spirit is.

The concept of an immortal soul comes from ancient Greek philosophers, particularly Plato. The Hellenistic view was that upon death the soul is freed from the body to an everlasting life of virtue, for good deeds done, or evil, for bad deeds committed.

The Bible makes no mention of an immortal soul. It is the spirit of man which is immortal.

It is this spirit of man – your higher consciousness – which is the master that must be raised from the shallow grave of your lower consciousness.

– 12 –
The doorway to your brain

The Tyler's job is to guard the outer door of the lodge. He observes the approach of cNegative thoughts damage both the physical body and the spiritowan's and eavesdroppers, and suffers none to pass, or re-pass, except such as are qualified and have permission from the Worshipful Master.

However, considering that Freemasonry is centred on the brain and its functions, and the brain is the house of your thoughts, what then is the true job of the Tyler? What part of the brain does he represent and what are his neurological functions?

Guardian of the brain

Should anyone argue that Freemasonry is not about the brain and its workings, they need only be directed to the ritual of opening a lodge in which the Tyler's jewel is defined in a dialogue between the Worshipful Master and the Junior Warden:

WM: Bro JW, the situation of the Tyler?

JW: Outside the door of the lodge.

WM: His duty?

JW: Being armed with a drawn sword to keep off all cowans and intruders to Freemasonry, and to see that the Candidates are properly prepared.

WM: What is the jewel of his office.

JW: The sword.

WM: What does it Masonically teach?

JW: To prevent the approach of *every unworthy thought*, and to *preserve a conscience* void of offence towards God and man.

Here the ritual quite clearly defines the role of the Tyler as a guardian not of the physical temple, but of the true temple of Masonic teaching – the brain and conscience. This is empirical proof that Masonic ritual concerns itself with neuroscience and morality. Our goal is to prevent the approach of every unworthy thought and preserve a conscience void of offence towards God and man, conscience defined as: *a person's moral sense of right and wrong, viewed as acting as a guide to one's behaviour.*

The sword, the spine, the skull

The use of the Tyler's sword dates back to the medieval operative craft guilds that closely guarded their trade secrets and posted a sentry outside meeting places to protect against intrusion from those unqualified.

The sentry, known as an outer guard, guarder, or doorkeeper, was often a junior apprentice lacking the qualifications to attend trade discussions.

When the operative guilds became speculative, the Tyler undertook the role of the outer guard.

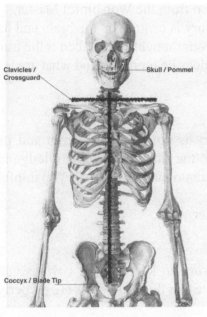

Clavicles / Crossguard

Skull / Pommel

Coccyx / Blade Tip

The Tyler's sword as the human skeleton, featuring the sword blade (spine) crossguard (clavicles) blade tip (coccyx) and pommel (skull).

The word 'Tyler' is old English for the doorkeeper of an inn. In the early days of English Freemasonry, lodges met in taverns and inns, and employed a Tyler to guard the doors of these establishments from those unqualified, malicious or curious.

As one who traditionally laid tiles on a roof, the Masonic Tyler sat on the roof of the lodge to prevent prying eyes catching a sneak peek through openings in the tiles. Sometimes the weight proved too much for the eaves and the curious onlooker would fall through the roof, hence the origin of the word 'eavesdropper.'

The jewel of the Tyler's office is a sword – a weapon to prevent unwanted advances towards the door of the lodge. However, as all is allegory and symbolism, and Freemasonry is neuroscience, we must consider the true meaning of the sword as the jewel of this office and how it relates to the brain.

A picture of the spine and brain reveals the symbolic Tyler's sword. See how the spinal cord resembles the blade of the sword, while the thalamus resembles the pommel at the top of the sword. In the picture of the skeleton, the spinal cord resembles the blade, the triangle-shaped coccyx resembles the point of the blade, the horizontal clavicles provide the crossguard, while the skull resembles the pommel at the top of the sword.

The brain stem that guards us

Offices of the lodge correspond to specific parts of the brain. The Tyler corresponds to the brain stem, at the entrance of the brain. Just as it is the Tyler's role to guard the lodge against Cowans and eavesdroppers, and to prevent the advance of every unworthy thought, so too is it the job of the brain stem to protect us when we perceive a threat.

In his 1990 book, *The Triune Brain in Evolution,* American physician and neuroscientist Paul D. MacLean explains that the triune brain consists of:

1. The reptilian complex (brain stem)
2. The paleo-mammalian complex (limbic system)
3. The neo-mammalian complex (neocortex)

The brain stem is incapable of sophisticated thought or emotional complexity. It controls our primitive instincts, including metabolic functions such as breathing, heart rate, blood pressure, digestion and arousal (being awake and alert).[39]

When our brain perceives a threat, our body retreats to the protection of the brain stem. Via the brain stem our breathing and heart rate quickens, our blood vessels constrict, our neck and chest tighten, our pupils dilate, and we may experience tunnel vision.

Just as the Tyler protects the lodge, the brain stem protects the brain from perceived exterior threats. Once again, we see proof of the neuroscience of Freemasonry.

A conscience void of...

Freemasonry is neuroscience and moral science; esoteric and exoteric. We have discovered the physical/neurological function of the Tyler and will now examine the office's moral function.

To understand the symbolism of the Tyler, think of him as a bouncer on the door of an exclusive club, being your inner self.

Tyling a lodge is the first great care of Masons when convened, which offers an indication as to the importance of the tyling process.

If you are the lodge and the lodge is you, it is imperative that you guard your mind against the entry of anything unworthy of admittance, or as the ritual states, against every unworthy thought. This doesn't mean to physically hold a sword and fend off people unworthy of being in your life. Rather the lesson here is to guard your thoughts against negativity. You must tyle your mind and keep your thoughts pure and positive, permitting entry only to those thoughts with positive influence. Use your personal Tyler to ensure that your thoughts are pure and unpolluted.

Negative thoughts damage both the physical body and the mind. The mind, body, and spirit are connected. As above, so below. Negative thoughts impact the physical body and cause sickness. You can literally think yourself ill! A study published in the *American Journal of Cardiology* claims that people with a high level of stress have a 27 percent higher risk of developing coronary heart disease.[40]

Superstitions, which are thought processes, may also deteriorate the body. Why is this? Because a person who believes in superstition impacts their health through negative beliefs.

Negative thoughts feed the amygdala, which is a mass of nuclei located in the temporal lobes of the brain near the hippocampus. Stimulation of the amygdala causes intense emotion, such as aggression or fear. The amygdala reacts to negative thoughts in various ways, including the activation of your sympathetic nervous system. This process is almost incomprehensibly quick. While it takes you around 300 milliseconds to become aware of a disturbing thought, the amygdala reacts to such thoughts in around 20 milliseconds!

A negative thought acts as a red flag to the amygdala, which sends out an alert that activates the brain's stress response, otherwise known as fight or flight response. The amygdala receives perceptual information related to external threats. When it interprets something as a danger, the amygdala sends signals to the brain's command centre, the hypothalamus. When the nervous system operates in flight or fight mode, the body's self-repair mechanisms function improperly, and the body becomes exposed to sickness.

Reality originates in the mental. Therefore, you have no greater goal as a human being than self-mastery, which, in essence, is mastery over your thoughts, which in turn leads to the illumination of your divine spark, or a shift to higher consciousness.

What you think manifests in your physical reality. Through your thoughts you attract and resist. Awareness of every thought, therefore, is of the greatest importance. How you shape your mind and use your mental energy – where you place the Tyler upon the boundaries of your thinking to determine your thought patterns – creates your existence.

Disquiet of the mind

As tyling the lodge is the first great care of Masons when convened, tyling your mind should be your first care before attempting any further advancement in personal betterment. The problem is, of course, that in the beginning of any work on ourselves the greatest hurdle we experience is our innate disquiet of mind.

How many times have you failed to fall asleep when your body is tired because your mind just won't quit? Your eyes and muscles are heavy but your mind (soul) is in its own world, happily thinking this and that while your tired body begs for it to shut up.

The mind by its very nature is erratic and unconstrained. To achieve self-improvement and become aware of your inner self requires a hushed and focused mind, free from negative emotions and the distractions of material things. Once again, picture King Solomon at the grave of GMHA and his words before raising the master: *My mind is now clear.*

To reach the state of consciousness and awareness to attain this clarity of mind, you need willpower and the ability to direct the mind towards your end aim, which is the illumination of your divine spark, your centre, your higher self: a shift to higher consciousness. You need to safeguard your mind against preoccupation with material possessions, ego, lusts and desires, and stop the mental processes that cause disharmony. As Jesus instructed his disciples, so too must you cast your net to the right, away from the clutter of the left brain.

Negative to positive

The process of changing the way you think – casting your net to the right, not the left – begins with changing your mindset. This change of mindset is applied by redirecting the flow of negativity (left side of the boat) into a flow of positivity (right side of the boat) through your reaction to daily events.

You cannot always control the events that impact your life, but you can control your reactions to events. You must realise that you cannot change the past and it is a waste of precious energy to obsess over the future. One is written into the annals of time and gone forever; the other never comes. You can only live in the present.

Negative thoughts enter your mind more often than not because you are preoccupied with the past or the future – both of which you cannot change in the present, which is the only place in which you exist. Ultimately the future and the past only exist as mental projections. They have no reality beyond the way in which your mind contemplates them and plays them over and over again. By attuning your mind to the present, you will eliminate the guilt and resentment of the past and the worry of the future, both of which cannot be altered in the present.

You are capable of altering the vibrational frequency of your thoughts to change yourself and your surroundings. When faced with anxiety, realise that for anxiety to exist in a world of dualities so too must calmness exist. Through positive thinking you can shift your mental fingers from a minor chord to a major chord, just as a pianist shifts fingers on a keyboard. If you can recognise the negative vibration (the pole of anxiety), you are capable of transmuting it into a positive vibration (the pole of calmness).

What you think manifests physically. A perfectly balanced state of mind leads to a perfect objective manifestation in the body and your surroundings. When your mind is unbalanced, you will manifest forms and ways that are detrimental not just to yourself, but to all those around you.

Use your inner Tyler to restore balance in your life and protect you against the unwanted advance of Cowans and eavesdroppers (negative thoughts).

– 13 –
Masonic G:
your second brain

Science has only recently 'discovered' something mystery schools have known for centuries: you actually have two brains, one in your head, the other in your solar plexus, which is the location of Freemasonry's letter 'G'.

Masonic ritual tells us the letter G stands for 'God,' 'Geometry' and the 'Great Geometrician of the Universe'. It is placed in the centre of the square and compasses, which are symbolic of you: the compasses represent your spiritual/higher self, sitting above the square, which is symbolic of your material self. The placement of the G at the centre represents the divine spark at your centre, or your connection to Supreme Consciousness.

Getting to the guts of 'G'

It is no coincidence that G is the seventh letter of the English alphabet. The number seven has long been considered a sacred number in Freemasonry, certain religions, and ancient mystery schools.

- Energy rises through seven chakras in the body, the seventh being the highest
- God created the world in six days and rested on the seventh
- Solomon's Temple took seven years to complete
- There are seven days in a week
- Seven notes to the diatonic scale
- Seven planets of the ancients moving in perfect harmony through the vast expanse of the universe
- Seven Sages of Ancient Greece
- Seven Wonders of the World
- Seven Liberal Arts and Sciences
- Seven stages of the alchemical process
- It takes seven Freemasons to make a lodge perfect
- Seven colours of the rainbow
- Seven continents on Earth
- In the Book of Revelation there are seven churches, seven seals,

seven trumpets, seven thunders, and the seven last plagues
- Seven is the sum of the spiritual (3/triangle) and material (4/square)
- Shakespeare's seven ages of man
- Seven candles of the Jewish Menorah
- Seven paths to heaven in ancient Egypt

G is the seventh letter of the English alphabet, and the third (3) letter of both the Greek alphabet (Gamma) and Hebrew alphabet (Gimmel). This is important to note as much Masonic symbolism derives from the ancient mystery schools, of which Greek and Hebrew were alphabets in employment.

The New Testament authors also wrote in Greek, which was the language of scholarship during the years the New Testament was written, from 50 to 100 CE.

Around 300 BCE the Old Testament was translated from Hebrew to Greek. This Greek translation, known as the Septuagint, was widely accepted and used in many synagogues.[41]

The writers of the New Testament sought to reach a broad, non-Israelite (Gentile) audience with their writings. Greek was the leading written and spoken language of the eastern Mediterranean region at the time and remained the dominant language in the Roman Empire for centuries. Jewish historian Josephus (37-100 CE) wrote that the ability to speak Greek was common among the general populous, slaves and servants.[42]

The fact that G represents two sacred numbers – 7 and 3 – makes it an even more extraordinary letter with great symbolic significance. It is no coincidence that the Masonic square resembles the number 7 when written as an inverted L. The same symbol in reverse is the Gamma (G) of the Greek alphabet. The symbol for Yod in the Hebrew alphabet also resembles the number 7. Yod is the tenth letter of the Hebrew alphabet and it is from Yod that all other letters of the alphabet are constructed. Symbolically, Yod represents God, as from God – Supreme Consciousness – all things are created. Written Yod also looks like a candle flame, representative of your divine spark.

Freemasonry places the letter G in the centre of the square and compasses, which is exactly where it needs to be to represent the divine spark at your centre. Elevation of this divine spark – your connection to Supreme Consciousness – is the end aim of Freemasonry's teachings. When you understand that the G represents your divine spark, the perfect god-part at your centre which is an inextinguishable flame, its depiction inside the square and compasses (or inside an equilateral triangle or blazing star) makes complete sense.

Ritual tells us G also symbolises Geometry, which we are taught is synonymous with Freemasonry. This is true if one starts with the science of Geometry and then delves deeper. Freemasonry teaches through Geometry that the student may curiously trace Nature through her various windings to her *most concealed recesses*.

This is a most important part of the ritual. We have just been taught that through Geometry – or Freemasonry, one being the same as the other – we are able to reveal the innermost parts of nature. This happens through a winding movement, represented by the winding staircase of the Fellowcraft degree. Similarly, the letter G winds by design. Through Freemasonry (Geometry) we're able to arrive at the very centre of our nature – our divine spark, or our inextinguishable spark of Supreme Consciousness.

Geometry is a precise science. Does the letter G lead us to a precise location for the centre of our being where the divine spark is located?

The answer is not revealed until the degrees of the Holy Royal Arch (York Rite) and Royal Arch of Solomon (Scottish Rite King of the Ninth Arch).

These degrees are designed around the building of the second Temple in Jerusalem, the first Temple, King Solomon's Temple, having been destroyed by Nebuchadnezzar II after the Siege of Jerusalem in 587 BCE. The Second Temple stood on the Temple Mount between 516BCE and 70CE when it was destroyed by the Romans.

While excavating the ground beneath King Solomon's original Temple, workmen discover an underground vault built by the prophet Enoch, constructed of nine arches, one on top of the other. Inside the ninth and innermost vault, Enoch placed a cubical block of marble in which he set a triangular plate of gold encrusted with precious stones and engraved with the ineffable name of God.

It is important to stress here that the story of Enoch's vaults is allegorical. There never was an actual physical vault with an actual physical marble block beneath an actual physical Solomon's Temple.

Enoch's vaults lead the workmen to uncover a great hidden treasure: the true name of God. However, this is not a literal name like John or Chris. The name of God is the essence of God, and that essence of God is the divine spark. To reach the hidden treasure, one must travel through the nine arches?

What are the nine arches?

The nine arches are the human ribs. Just above the ninth set of ribs is located a horizontal line known as the transplyoric plane. At the centre of this plane is located the solar plexus, which is also known as the second brain.

On the website www.learning-mind.com we find information on the solar plexus as the second brain:

Starting from the same tissues, the brain and the stomach originate and basically decide to take two separate roads of development, or the great creator programs this move. Either way, two paths originate and split to govern two separate areas of the body. This is where the material changes to form our brain, the central nervous system and stomach, the enteric nervous system. The interesting aspect of this split revolves around the Vagus nerve. The Vagus nerve connects the two nervous systems for life. Because of this connection, both the brain and the gut share neurotransmitters and hormones.

On the website www.spiritscience.net, an article by LJ Vanier informs us:

Dubbed "The Second Brain" by Michael Gershon, Chairman of the Department of Anatomy and Cell Biology at New York–Presbyterian Hospital/Columbia University Medical Center. The network of neurons that line our guts are filled with (over 100 million) neurotransmitters which to put it simply, do a lot more than simply digest our food.

'What Gershon found is that the enteric nervous system directly connects to the larger central system at the base of the skull, that assists in feeding information to our brains through the hypothalamus and pituitary, known as the Gut Brain Axis. This information exchange then helps to determine our mental state, as well as playing a crucial role when it comes to disease in the body.

'While this second brain has not been proven to formulate its own conscious thought, nor play any major role in our decision-making process, "The system is way too complicated to have evolved only to make sure things move out of your colon," says Emeran Mayer, professor of physiology, psychiatry and biobehavioral sciences at the David Geffen School of Medicine at the University of California, Los Angeles (UCLA).

New Thought lecturer, Julia Seton, says:

The Solar Plexus is the home of the ego or the spirit of men; it is the connecting link between man and the Infinite and is the meeting place of the divinely physical, and the physically divine man. From the solar plexus we receive our visions called faith, and when we register them in the field of consciousness of our physical brain and work them out through scientific human reasoning into tangible expression, they then become facts.[43]

American New Thought author, Theron Q. Dumont, tells us that we have mistaken our heart as the seat of our emotions, whereas really our emotions stem from the solar plexus:

One of the great facts concerning the Solar Plexus, or Abdominal Brain...which has been known for centuries by occultists...is this important fact, i.e. that the Solar Plexus is the seat of the emotional nature of Man. In short, that the part popularly held to be played by 'the heart' is in reality performed by the Solar Plexus.[44]

The third chakra (number 3/letter G) is also located at the solar plexus. The most common Sanskrit name for this chakra is Manipura, which means 'city of jewels' or 'seat of gems'. According to chakra anatomy, the message of the third chakra is: 'You have the power to choose.' And what is the power of choice otherwise known as? Consciousness.

Manipura is associated with inner wisdom, self-confidence, and is also called the 'lion's centre', which links us back to the symbolism of the Lion of the tribe of Judah as discussed earlier in this book.

The letter G in the centre of the square and compasses, we have now learned, is a clear message that we have a divine spark at our centre. To activate this divine spark is to raise your consciousness and reconnect with Supreme Consciousness. Freemasonry is a key to unlocking and activating the divine spark. As Masonic author Albert Pike wrote: 'Freemasonry is the subjugation of the Human that is in man by the Divine.'

PART 2

The Exoteric
Freemasonry's moral science as a path to the highest kind of oneness

– 14 –
Want vs Desire: why you must knock on the door

Freemasonry requires the candidate for initiation to knock at its door. Nobody else can knock for the candidate, he must do so himself, and for a very important reason.

There are prerequisites to becoming a Freemason. One must approach the lodge of his 'own free will and accord,' that is, he must enter into Freemasonry of his own desire and not at the behest or compulsion of anyone else.

A candidate must be a 'free man'. The term 'free' here refers to the candidate's freedom to choose to become a Freemason. A free man is not coerced into Freemasonry, he has freely made his own choice to join the fraternity and is free to formulate his own opinion of Freemasonry. Writes Lloyd Hussey: 'But, we are also masons, "being free", that is, not subject to the orders or mandates of any person in our decisions to join Freemasonry, nor bullied, nor blackmailed, nor coerced, nor bribed, not browbeaten, nor badgered into our decisions, but rather, freely, of our own free will and accord did we make the decision.'[45]

To journey on the path to heightened consciousness, the candidate will need to free himself from avarice, lust, and the shackles of the ego that binds him to his left brain thinking, his material/animal/lower nature. Freedom from this aspect of himself is symbolised by the removal of the cable tow from around the candidate's neck.

The cable tow
Nikola Tesla said: 'It is only through enlightenment that we become conscious of our limitations.' The cable tow represents our limitations, and its removal is symbolic of attaining enlightenment.

Though purely Masonic in its current use, the cable tow is rooted in antiquity. The cable tow's function in initiation into ancient mystery schools stemmed in part from man's use of ropes to domesticate animals. Ropes were first fashioned to bring wild beasts under control and thus came to symbolise mastery over brute nature. When the animal was able to control its own behaviour, the rope was removed. Removal of the rope in initiatory practices signified transcendence of the brute self into a higher state of existence in which one experienced self-control and governance from within. Behaviour and actions were no longer influenced by reactions to the external but were a response to the internal.

Life in a material world forces a cable tow around our necks. The followers of Zoroaster believe that everyone has a noose around their neck which, upon death, falls off those who lived a righteous (illuminated) life or drags the evil doer to hell.

The Masonic cable tow is symbolic of the bind material life puts on the individual. Its removal symbolises the removal of the tie to your lower nature, which is the crudest version of you; unrefined, rough, primitive and unaltered by any processing. The lowest self is centred on the ego, which is made up of such components as: pride, guilt, aggression, elitism, illusion, denial, conformity, boredom, the need for attention and validation, conditional love, skepticism, hostility, and the failure to realise the divinity in oneself.

You have a choice to succumb to your lower self or aspire to greater heights. Being a free man requires a belief that higher thoughts and a reconnection with Supreme Consciousness is achievable. One without such realisation is not a free man, as he will always be bound to his lower nature.

Well recommended is not enough

The candidate for Freemasonry must be 'well recommended', but recommendation alone does not guarantee admission into the Craft. The recommendation is only a suggestion or proposal put forward by an authoritative person, that is, one who is already a Master Mason. I have seen plenty of well recommended men fall short of initiation into Freemasonry.

Most importantly, the candidate for Freemasonry must be desirous of receiving initiation, the word 'desirous' being of particular importance. The Candidate should not 'want' initiation, he must *desire* initiation.

'Want' and 'desire' are words used interchangeably by most of us to refer to the same thing even though there is a subtle difference between both. The difference between want and desire is the degree of longing.

Wanting something is a simple need for something that we do not already possess. Desire is a more intense craving for someone or something. Desire is stronger and more intense than want and continues to grow for a longer period in comparison to want, which is usually fleeting in duration.

Want constantly changes. For example, right now I want a cup of coffee because I do not have one in my possession. In ten minute's time, I may feel like a glass of water instead of coffee, and thus my want for coffee is gone.

A desire is more intense than a want, and the craving for whatever one desires will usually last a lot longer than a want. For example, if I desire to learn to play the guitar, I will dedicate time, enthusiasm and hard work to achieve this desire.

The candidate for Freemasonry should not want to be a Freemason, he should desire to be so.

Desire is all important

Why must the candidate desire initiation, and not simply 'want' it? As Freemasonry is brain science, we will find the answer to this question in the brain's energy output.

The human brain is both a transmitter and receiver of frequency. The frequencies transmitted by the brain are capable of changing one's environment, including changing physical matter and influencing other people. According to Freemason Thomas Edison, when great focus is placed on the frequencies emitted by our brains, those frequencies pass through the ether and are able to be received by other human brains and affect other physical matter. These frequencies travel faster than the speed of light and are capable of being received instantaneously by brains on the other side of the planet.

Have you ever desired someone to call you? Suddenly your phone rings and, lo and behold, it is the very person to whom your desire was directed? That's a small example of what Edison was talking about.

Now consider this: if the desire for someone to call you is a result of focusing your brain's frequency output in a small way, what could be accomplished with greater focus of your brain's transmitting frequencies?

Good vibrations

Japanese author, photographer and entrepreneur, Masaru Emoto, researched the effect of human consciousness on the molecular structure of water.

Emoto's early work revolved around pseudoscientific hypotheses that water could react to positive thoughts and words, both spoken and written, and that polluted water could be cleaned through prayer and positive visualisation, or the power of positive thoughts.

Emoto played music to tap water and discovered that doing so produced beautiful crystal formations in the frozen water. He wrote messages such as 'I love you' on one bottle of water and 'I hate you' on another bottle of water and discovered that the positively labeled bottle produced gorgeous crystal formations, while the negatively labeled bottle caused ugly, distorted crystals or no crystals at all. When he prayed for the water or sent it loving thoughts, that is, when his brain transmitted and focused on positive frequencies, beautiful frozen water crystals began to appear in tap water.

If Emoto achieved these results with positive/negative thoughts directed towards basic tap water, imagine the effects of positive/negative thoughts on the water in your body, particularly the water in your brain. Imagine how your thoughts can affect the water in other people's brains. Actually, you don't have to imagine, you just have to remember how it felt the last time somebody told you they hated you or called you fat, a loser, a snob, a bitch, a bastard, or any other derogatory remark. Not so good, right? But when someone tells you they love you, you did great work, or they're proud of you, you feel on top of the world!

The bottom line is that there is evidence of the human brain transmitting frequencies that affect physical matter.

If thoughts (frequencies) are powerful enough to alter matter, they can also alter non-matter, that is, alter ourselves and those around us in an unphysical/spiritual/discarnate way.

Define your desire

Self-help author Napoleon Hill said that the key to success is to define your dream. You need to clearly know what you want, and for that want to come true requires a burning desire.

Long before Napoleon Hill spoke of such things in the 1950s, Freemasonry taught the same lesson. At the commencement of any of degree, the candidate is introduced to the lodge as: 'A poor blind candidate, who is *desirous* of having and receiving a part in the rights, lights, and benefits of this Worshipful Lodge of Free and Accepted Masons.'

The word 'desirous' is important here. The candidate does not want the rights, lights or benefits, he is *desirous* of such. To want something transmits a weak vibration from the brain, but to desire something, to truly and utterly need it in your life, sends out a strong, determined vibration that lets the universe know this is the direction you're telling your life to take. The more you desire something the stronger you think about it; the more you think about it, the more that desire broadcasts a strong transmission to the listening, responsive universe that what you desire should somehow come into your possession/experience.

This is why a Freemason is first made so in his heart – the location of desire.

This is why the Secretary asks the candidate prior to his admission into the lodge: 'Do you seriously declare, upon your honour, that unbiased by the improper solicitation of friends, and uninfluenced by mercenary motives, you freely and voluntarily offer yourself a candidate for the mysteries of Freemasonry?'

This is why the candidate must be free born; free to make his own choice, to transmit his burning desire for initiation into Freemasonry.

The candidate must knock on the door himself three times as an expression of his desire. Nobody else can knock for him as nobody will ever have the zeal or desire for yourself that you do.

– 15 –
A Freemason is straight up

'He's straight up.'
   'He's a stand up guy.'
   How many times have you heard these two phrases? Their use has become part of our vernacular for describing someone who is honest in their dealings and unwavering in their positive intent. But did you know that the terms 'straight up' and 'stand up' come from Freemasonry?
   One of the three working tools of the Fellowcraft is a plumb, also known as a plumb-line or plumb-rule. A builder's tool used to construct a perfect perpendicular, the plumb's symbolic use is some of the most important in all of Freemasonry.
   A plumb is a lead weight attached to a string. It is used by builders and carpenters to establish a perfect vertical or perpendicular. In other words, a plumb determines how straight (up and down) something is.
   The term 'plumb' is often used in sports such as cricket when a batsman is dismissed for LBW (Leg Before Wicket). The ball hits his straight leg in front of the wicket and he is therefore declared 'out plumb'. When a boxer lands a clean knockout punch to an opponent's chin or bloodies his nose with a perfect jab or cross, he is said to have 'caught him plumb,' alluding to the perfection of the blow.
   The ritual of the Fellowcraft degree tells us: 'The plumb admonishes us to walk uprightly in our several stations before God and man.'
   Pretty simple, right? The plumb measures uprights, and therefore symbolises our own uprightness. Lesson learned, nothing more to see here.
   On the contrary! There is a lot more to this seemingly simple tool.

Amos, what seest thou?
During the second degree, the Holy Bible is opened at Amos 7:7-8 in which Amos receives a vision of God sitting on a wall with a plumb in His hand.
   Who was Amos?
   Regarded as one of twelve minor prophets, Amos lived in the village of Tekoah, on the Eastern slopes of the Judean hills, about eight kilometres

south of Bethlehem, during the 8th century BCE. Before becoming a prophet, he worked as a shepherd and a sycamore fig farmer.

During this time the tribes of Israel were under the reign of King Jeroboam II, who ruled for forty years. He reclaimed all lands that had been lost by his predecessors and captured parts of Syria including its capital, Damascus. Jeroboam II also repaired much of the damage his father had done to the Southern Kingdom of Judah and gave part of the land he had taken from Syria to the King of Judah, Amatziah.

This was a period of tremendous prosperity for the Northern Kingdom and its people, who traded with the seafaring Phoenicians and imported luxury items to lavish their lifestyles. With an increase in riches came a fall in moral standards and a rise in idolatry. The poor were oppressed and the rich no longer sought the wisdom of the Torah.

It was during this period of moral decay for the Northern Kingdom that Amos had his vision. Mind you, Amos was just one of many prophets at the time. God, it seemed, was using all kinds of messengers to tell people to start behaving or suffer the consequences!

Amos 7:7-8 reads:

> *Thus he shewed me; and behold the Lord stood upon a wall made by a plumb-line, with a plumb-line in His hand. And the Lord said unto me, Amos, what seest thou? And I said, A plumb-line. Then said the Lord: Behold, I will set a plumb-line in the midst of my people Israel. I will not again pass by them any more.*

Let's get a variant from the New Century Version (NCV) Bible:

> *This is what he showed me: The Lord stood by a straight wall, with a plumb-line in His hand. The Lord said to me, "Amos, what do you see?" I said, "A plumb-line." Then the Lord said, "See, I will put a plumb-line among my people Israel to show how crooked they are. I will not look the other way any longer."*

The Moral Law

Those are strong words from God. He's upset and He's going to start dishing out severe punishment to the wicked. He won't tolerate the decay of moral standards any longer.

The wall God sits upon isn't a physical wall. God's wall represents the laws and commandments set down by Him for all humanity to live by. The plumb-line in God's hand alludes to the strict code of morals He expects from us, and the complete and absolute justice He will impose upon any who live immorally. In capitulating to their animal natures in the pursuit of purely materialistic lifestyles, the people had defied the moral law.

We each have the power of personal choice; every situation can proceed in adherence to the moral law or against the moral law. The choice is yours! If you choose to defy the moral law – the Universal Law that binds all beings, which forms the framework of society and holds it together – you're going to suffer some terrible consequences.

Be a good person. It's that simple!

The sixth Hermetic principle

Every cause has its effect; every effect has its cause; everything happens according to law; chance is but a name for law not recognised; there are many planes of causation but nothing escapes the law no matter the plane of causation.

This is the sixth Hermetic principle (The Principle of Cause and Effect) as described in *The Kybalion*. It is the *kamma* (karma in Sanskrit) of Buddhism; the causality of Aristotle's *Physics,* and Isaac Newton's *Rule of Reasoning in Philosophy.* Through an understanding of cause and effect, we learn to take charge of our actions in order to serve our own welfare as well as to promote the welfare of others. Good actions and bad actions will produce their respective pleasant and painful effects regardless of the ideology and aspirations of the people who engage in them. To put it simply: stuff happens as a result of stuff you do. Do good stuff and good stuff happens in return. Do bad stuff and you get an angry God sitting on a wall with a plumb-line in His hand.

'I will not pass by them any more'

Amos 7:8 may be a little confusing at first glance when God says, 'I will not pass them by them any more.' This should be interpreted as God being exasperated with the immoral ways of His people. In other words, He's sick and tired of their shenanigans and is unwilling to turn a blind eye. He will start meting out punishment, and that punishment will be severe.

The *Modern Living Bible* phrases it best: 'I will test my people with a plumb-line. I will no longer turn away from punishing.'

God is telling Amos that from this point on, He demands that His people walk justly and uprightly in rectitude and truth, without even the slightest deviation from the path of virtue.

As children it was our parents who set their plumb-line among us, teaching us how to live, sometimes looking the other way when we acted out, putting our behaviour down to a lack of knowing right from wrong. Such excuses are intolerable in adulthood. An adult takes responsibility for his actions. God showing Amos a plumb-line is the equivalent of Him saying, 'Grow up and stop acting like a child!'

When you begin to achieve uprightness, using your plumb-line to test the wall of your character, the reward is advanced knowledge.

This knowledge comes from within, from the divine spark at your centre that connects you to the Source. It is the fire in your belly, the potential that exists in all life forms but is hidden by our animal nature. It is what Jesus spoke of when he said, 'The kingdom of God is within you.' It is as described in Ecclesiastes 3:11: 'He hath made every thing beautiful in his time: also he hath set the world in their heart, so that no man can find out the work that God maketh from the beginning to the end.'

Your purpose in life is not revealed to you as writing on a chalkboard. To find your purpose you must elevate yourself above the mundane, toward a reconnection with the universe, the centre, the source, whatever you wish to call it.

Recognising your divine spark

Recognising your divine spark is a common theme throughout religions of the world and various teaching systems, including yoga in which practitioners greet each other with the word 'namaste'.

'Namaste' is a form of greeting commonly employed by Hindus. The word is accompanied by a gesture whereby the hands are placed together between the eyes, where the internal 'third eye' is located, then dropped (along a straight vertical – the plumb line) to the centre of the chest where the heart is located. This gesture, known as Anjali Mudra or pranamasana translates as, 'I bow to the divine in you.'[46] It recognises the belief that the divine spark in me is the same in all. We are all connected to a greater intelligence, Supreme Consciousness, through our centre.

The self we parade through life, which reflects in the mirror, is but an adaptation to our environment. You may think it's the real you, but it isn't. It is the earthly you. Just as the seed's purpose is to grow into a mighty upright oak, so within you is the means to grow into a mighty upright being. The choice is yours to make.

You may choose to elevate yourself above your base nature and be upright in your thoughts and actions, or you may choose to exhibit no uprightness in life. But if you do choose the latter, be prepared for the consequences that will come your way.

– 16 –
Are all present Freemasons?

There's an old saying: it's hard to fly like an eagle when surrounded by turkeys. Freemasons understand this, which is why before the opening of any Masonic lodge a check is done to ensure that everyone in the room is a Freemason.

One of the most asked questions a Freemason receives from members of the general public is: what exactly do you guys do inside your lodge room? Explaining every detail of what goes on inside a lodge would take pages, but an easy partial answer to this question is: first, we make sure that everyone present is a Freemason.

The opening of a Masonic lodge is an important ritual that seeks to accomplish many things. These include the establishment of harmony among its members and the recognition of every lodge officer being in their rightful place and fully aware of the operative and symbolic duties of their office. However, before any of these processes commence, the Master of the lodge must first establish that everyone in the room is a Freemason.

'Are all present Masons?' the Worshipful Master asks the Senior Warden.

The Senior Warden responds that he will 'ascertain through the proper officers and report,' upon which he summons the two Deacons. The Senior Warden sends the Deacons up and down both sides of the lodge room, whereby they inspect every person to ensure they are wearing an apron. If a visitor is present, the Deacon may do a quick inspection to establish their Masonic credentials, but this process usually takes place before the lodge is opened by a small investigative team.

As you can see, Freemasons place great importance on making sure that once the doors to their lodge room close, everyone inside that room is a Freemason.

Why is this?

Anti-Freemasons are quick to assume that this process is performed out of the need for secrecy in a Masonic lodge. After all, inside the lodge room is where those dastardly Freemasons plot the takeover of the world, control the banks and hide the alien bodies, right?

Sorry to smash your tin-foil hats, but the reason why the Worshipful Master of the lodge ensures that all present are Freemasons before commencing any business is because Freemasons value the company of like-minded men.

The company you keep

The importance of good company is essential to success.[47] We are individuals, but our journey through life interacts with others. The last thing you want on that path is a bunch of hangers-on slowing you down and complaining that their feet are sore, they need a smoke break, and they'll sit back while you do all the hard work. Life is a shared experience, but we must be selective about who we share that experience with if we are to reap its greatest benefit. After all, a lion doesn't hunt alongside an antelope, and an Olympic trap shooter doesn't practice alongside a hillbilly popping tin cans off a fence with his BB gun.

American entrepreneur, Jim Rohn, says: 'You are the average of the five people you spend the most time with.'[48] This is debatable because it doesn't factor in the person you actually spend the most time with – yourself. But Rohn makes an interesting point: the people you surround yourself with have a major impact on your life. Therefore, every effort should be taken to spend your time with people who will enhance and enrich your life.

They don't have to be saints, but they need to be people who won't suck the goodness out of your life and will help your inner light shine as much as you will help their own light shine.

American judge, Charles Evan Hughes, said: 'A man has to live with himself, and he should see to it that he always has good company.' Here Hughes is talking about the company of the self, which is just as important as the company of others. We all live with and inside of ourselves – there's no escape. Through constant self-betterment – mentally, physically and spiritually – we improve the person we keep the most company with: ourselves. The Masonic lodge room is symbolic of a person. Its various officers symbolise the components that make up the individual brain.

Therefore, when the Deacons inspect the room to make sure all present are Freemasons, they are not only checking whether everyone is on the same page as individuals comprising a group, they are symbolically ensuring that the individual mind is keeping good company with the individual brain and the individual spirit.

Harmony is key

One of the keys to personal happiness is harmony. If any one of your three aspects are out of whack, or if you carry more yin than yang, the consequences detract from your personal harmony, and there is little joy in leading a disharmonious life. You can be the guy who goes to the gym twice a day, follows a strict paleo diet and is a shining example of physical well-being. But if you're going home to an empty house with no company in your life because your personality is abrasive and uncongenial, you're living in disharmony.

Freemasons know the importance of surrounding themselves with good people, but this doesn't mean that everyone in the lodge room shares the same likes and dislikes. What it does mean is that every Freemason in that lodge room is walking the same path of self-improvement.

Freemasonry is an organisation that seeks to make good men better. When you're in a lodge room there is a common feeling that you're there with like-minded individuals who are seeking to better themselves. That may be where the commonality ends, which is not a bad thing! Surrounding yourself with good people doesn't mean you have to surround yourself with similar people. In fact, too much of the same inhibits personal growth. Variety really is the spice of life. We're not sheep in a flock blindly following the shepherd from one patch of grass to another. We're singers, dancers, musicians, directors and stage-hands in the play of life all performing our parts to create a beautiful and rewarding experience.

Karl Marx said: 'Surround yourself with people who make you happy. People who make you laugh, who help you when you're in need. People who genuinely care. They are the ones worth keeping in your life. Everyone else is just passing through.'

Your vibrational state

Someone once said to me, 'We become the company we keep'. I understood this concept but never fully realised how true it was until I became a father.

My wife likes to call my son my 'mini-me'. When I blow my nose, he pretends to blow his nose. When I yawn, he pretends to yawn. When I'm chatting on the phone, he pretends to chat on an invisible phone. In short, he is being shaped as a person by the company he keeps in these formative years, and that company is me. This realisation struck me like a lightning bolt. Keeping good company is not a one-way street! What you put out is what you receive. Like attracts like. My vibrational state directly affects the vibrational state of those in my company, and vice versa.

What do I mean by vibrational state? Let's look at the Kybalion?

Originally published in 1912, *The Kybalion* was written by three unknown authors under the pseudonym 'The Three Initiates'. It claims to be the teachings of Hermetic philosophy and details Seven Principles by which the entire universe is governed. This philosophy is said to be the essence of the teachings of Hermes Trismegistus (thrice-great Hermes), the purported author of the *Hermetic Corpus*, a series of sacred texts that are the basis of Hermeticism.

It is debated as to whether Hermes was, in fact, Greek or Egyptian and whether or not he was an actual physical person at all or rather a conscious energy construct without a body. Interestingly, the celebrated American psychic, Edgar Cayce, claimed in some of his trance readings that Hermes or Thoth (the Egyptian moon good) was an engineer from the submerged Atlantis, who also built, designed or directed the construction of the pyramids of Egypt.[49]

The third Hermetic principle is the Principle of Vibration: 'Nothing rests; everything moves; everything vibrates.'

Write the authors of *The Kybalion*:

> *From corpuscle and electron, atom and molecule, to worlds and universes, everything is in vibratory motion. This is also true on the planes of energy and force (which are but varying degrees of vibration); and also on the mental planes (whose states depend upon vibrations); and even on to the spiritual planes.*

An understanding of this principle, with the appropriate formulas, enables Hermetic students to control their own mental vibrations as well as those of others. The Masters also apply this principle to the conquering of natural phenomena, in various ways. 'He who understands the Principle of Vibration, has grasped the sceptre of power', says one of the old writers.

You have the power to change your vibrations, and as such attract positivity or negativity – success or failure; good people or bad people – into your life. Put simply, being a negative Nelly will attract other negative Nellies as misery loves company. If you're feeling miserable in the knowledge that the only people in your life are similarly miserable beings, you have the power to change your vibrations. How? Start with something so simple as a smile!

You're never fully dressed without a smile

Deliberately putting a smile on your face when you're not feeling happy can improve your mood. Fact! In 1990, facial coding expert Paul Ekman found that adopting a 'Duchenne smile' – a smile that raises the corners of the mouth and pushes up the cheeks, causing crow's feet around the eyes – produced a change in brain activity that induced a better mood in subjects.[50]

An article published in *Psychological Science* detailed research conducted by Tara Kraft and Sarah Pressman in which subjects performed stressful tasks while assuming neutral expressions and different smiles, some configured by using chopsticks in their mouths. Subjects who smiled were found to have lower heart rates than those who held neutral expressions. Those with Duchenne smiles were the most relaxed, and even those subjects with forced smiles reported feeling happier than those who didn't smile.[52]

Think about it for a moment: who do you keep company with? Are those people vibrating positively or negatively, and how is their vibrational level affecting your own energies? Think also about the company you keep inside yourself. Is that little voice in your head communicating dark, miserable, negative messages or happy, uplifting, positive messages?

If you want to be an eagle, don't surround yourself with turkeys, but also remember that life is reciprocal. Don't be a turkey if you want to soar with the eagles.

– 17 –
Take no short cuts

Masonic symbols import meaning to an embodiment of picture images and data within a specific school of thought[53]. Many of the symbols through which Freemasonry imparts its teachings are hundreds of years old; others are older than the pyramids!

Symbols within Masonic ritual were employed by the ancient Sumerians (approx. 3500 BCE), Phoenicians (approx. 1500 BCE), Persians (approx. 4000 BCE) and Mesopotamians (approx. 3100 BCE), and in the mystery schools of ancient Greece (approx. 530 BCE) and Egypt (approx. 3150 BCE).

Freemasonry is the only institution in the world that effectively carries an unbroken line of ancient mystery school teaching into the modern world. Masonic ritual tells us that the usages and customs among Freemasons:

> *...have ever borne a near affinity to those of the ancient Egyptians. Their philosophers, unwilling to expose their mysteries to vulgar eyes, couched their systems of learning and polity under signs and hieroglyphical figures, which were communicated to their chief priests or Magi alone, who were bound by solemn oath to conceal them. The system of Pythagoras was formed on a similar principle, as well as many others of more recent date. Masonry, however, is not only the most ancient but the most honourable society that ever existed, as there is not a character or emblem here depicted but serves to inculcate the principles of piety and virtue among all its genuine professors.*

The longevity of these symbols is proof to their effectiveness in conveying moral, philosophical, metaphysical and scientific lessons. Any lesser symbols would have died out hundreds, if not thousands of years ago.

Operative and Speculative

Carl Jung believed there are concepts beyond the human range of comprehension. No matter how much we think we know, there is a point we reach from which our conscious knowledge can go no further.[54] Symbols speak to a part of us beyond our conscious, pressing deeper into our psyche than words or actions.

Most Masonic symbols comprise two parts: the operative and the speculative. Operative refers to the actual physical purpose of the object depicted in the symbol. We see operative symbols around us every day. A handicap sign in a parking space; a traffic light; a seat belt sign on an airplane; a non-smoking sign; a smiley face emoticon. These are all operative symbols with no speculative aspect. Speculative symbolism refers to the philosophical or moral teaching of the object depicted in the symbol.

The Masonic symbol of a winding staircase is rich with meaning. Ritual tells us that a winding staircase rose from the ground floor of King Solomon's Temple to the Middle Chamber. There, after proving themselves with a series of secret handshakes and passwords, the workmen received their wages of corn, wine and oil; representative of nourishment, refreshment and joy.

First, Kings 6:8 states: 'The door for the middle chamber was in the right side of the house; and they went up with winding stairs into the middle chamber and out of the middle into the third.'

Was King Solomon's Temple an actual building? The Bible, like Freemasonry, uses allegory and symbolism to impart its teachings. As Paul said in Romans 2:29: 'We should serve in the newness of the Spirit and not in the oldness of the letter.' What he's basically saying is, look beyond the words (the letter) and embrace the spirit of what is being said. Likewise, the true lessons of Freemasonry are beyond the words.

If we accept the official line that Freemasonry is 'a beautiful system of morality, veiled in allegory and illustrated by symbols' then the building of King Solomon's Temple is a story used to impart an important lesson. It is an allegory; a literary device in which characters or events in a literary, visual or musical art form represent or symbolise ideas or concepts. An allegory conveys its hidden message through symbolic figures, actions, imagery and/or events. More concisely, an allegory is a story, poem, or picture which can be interpreted to reveal a hidden meaning, typically a moral or political one.

Beyond the words

The words are important, but beyond the words is where the true message lies. As author and Freemason Rudyard Kipling said: 'It is the inside meaning, not the words, that count.'

So, what is the true meaning of the Masonic winding stairs?

In the second degree lecture, the newly passed brother (he has symbolically 'passed' from the Ground Floor to the Middle Chamber; material to mental) is told: 'We are about to endeavour to work our way into a place representing the Middle Chamber of King Solomon's Temple...In doing this it will be necessary for us to make an advance, emblematically, through a porch, up a flight of winding stairs...'

Once again, this stair climb is completely symbolic. There is no actual winding staircase in the lodge room. What is important to note – perhaps more important than the staircase itself – is the fact that it winds. This begs the question: *wouldn't a straight staircase be quicker and more direct?*

The answer is yes. But sometimes you cannot get to where you want to go via a straight line. Think of it like driving up a mountain. You can't reach the summit by driving on a straight road. The only way to the top is to follow a road that winds up and around the mountain.

Specifically a winding staircase

Freemasonry is a progressive science. One does not come to a complete knowledge of Freemasonry in an instant, but rather through stages. The definition of 'progressive' is: 'Happening or developing gradually or in stages; proceeding step by step.' The progressive science of Freemasonry is a system of education that teaches self-improvement through a time-consuming process without quick fixes. If the Ground Floor represents the Mason as a child, reaching the Middle Chamber represents him as an adult. The path from childhood to adulthood is an educational process that takes on a spiral form.

Author Jerome Bruner details the idea of spiral curriculum in his 1960 book, *The Process of Education*. Spiral curriculum is a method of learning whereby subjects are broken into strands or ideas that are repeatedly taught to a child, year after year, with increasing levels of complexity. Spiral learning introduces a topic, touches on it for a short time and then moves on. The topic is revisited and expanded upon, with the student picking up more information the second time, then the third time, as around they go in a spiral. With each learning session, the student expands on their skill level and builds new understanding. The theoretical idea is that brief exposure to a topic, then revisiting it, allows students to construct their own understanding on a basic framework.

The spiral of life

It's only natural that our educational growth takes the form of a spiral. After all, we are a part of nature, and nature is spiral. Therefore, any processes we undertake, if in accordance to the nature of things, should be spiral in its makeup, not straight lined. Logarithmic spirals, as first described by Descartes, and the Fibonacci sequence (that approximates the golden mean spiral), is proof that spirality exists in nature.

The Fibonacci sequence is as follows:

0, 1, 1, 2, 3, 5, 8, 13, 21, 34, 55, 89, 144...

Put simply, you add the two previous numbers to receive the sum of the next number. Thus 0+1 = 1; 1+1 = 2; 2+1 = 3; 3+2 = 5 and so forth.

If one draws a tiling with squares whose side lengths are successive Fibonacci numbers, then draws arcs connecting the opposite corners of squares in the Fibonacci tiling, a Fibonacci spiral is created. Divide any number in the Fibonacci sequence by the one before it, for example 21/13 or 34/21, and the answer is always close to 1.61803. This is known as the Golden Ratio and from it we derive the Golden Mean Spiral (Golden Mean Geometry). The Golden Mean Spiral is considered the finger print of creation. The shape of hurricanes, sea shells, and the flight patterns of birds, including the approach of a hawk to its prey, are just a few examples of Golden Mean Spirals in nature. Even DNA molecules adhere to the spirality of nature.

The DNA molecule is 34 angstroms long by 21 angstroms wide for each full cycle of its double helix spiral. These are successive numbers in the Fibonacci sequence, meaning that our own DNA is based on the Golden Mean Spiral. When you consider that King Solomon's Temple is an allegory of the human body, specifically the human brain, you can't help but wonder if the winding staircase alludes to our DNA.

According to scientists, 15 percent of our DNA has not yet been decoded. This uncoded DNA could allow us to function higher than we currently do. Masonic ritual says that the winding staircase of the Temple numbered 3, 5 and 7 steps, the total of which is 15! Is the winding staircase an allusion to this 15 percent of DNA that may transform us above our current nature?

Spiralling your education puts you in harmony with the expansion process that is at the centre of creation. Just as nature grows spirally, so should our education take a spiral route. This is the heart of the lesson of the winding staircase. Don't take shortcuts.

True advancement requires a spiral ascension. Sure, you may think you're getting to a destination quicker via a straight line, but what you're really doing is taking a short cut. And if there is one thing you should never, ever cut short, it is your personal advancement. Taking short cuts leaves you short. Says best-selling author Orrin Woodard: 'There are many shortcuts to failure, but there are no shortcuts to true success.' To reach the top of the mountain, you must drive up and around. The winding staircase's spiral design tells us that our ascension in life must conform to the laws of all creation.

Not easy but necessary

Climbing a winding staircase isn't easy. Success comes from hard work with no short cuts taken. As alternate religions writer, Catherine Bayer, said: 'Each of us progresses from child to adult to old age. As such, the spiral is not a symbol of stagnation but rather of change, progression, and development. It embraces these things as good and healthy and helps one to accept change even though we often are more comfortable retreating into tradition and old, standard ways.'[55]

Prolific Masonic author, Albert Mackey, wrote in *The Symbolism of Freemasonry*:

> It is here that the intellectual education of the candidate begins... where childhood ends and manhood begins, he finds stretching out before him a winding stair which invites him, as it were, to ascend, and which as the symbol of discipline and instruction, teaches him that here he must commence Masonic labour – here he must enter upon those glorious though difficult researches, the end of which is to be the possession of divine truth... He cannot stand still if he would be worthy of his vocation; his destiny as an immortal being requires him to ascend, step by step, until the summit, where the treasures of knowledge await him.

Don't take shortcuts in life, especially when it comes to self-improvement. Accept that education is a spiral process, not a straight line, and ascend your own spiral staircase in confidence.

When you stand at the base of a winding staircase, your view of the top is hidden. You don't know what's around the bend. You need to have faith that although there may be personal struggles around those bends, which you can't yet see, climbing past these struggles will provide you with new experience. You're going to get to the top – to where you want to go. The only question is: will you take a short cut to get there or will you do the work, put in the hard yards, and make it worthwhile?

Einstein said: 'Genius is one percent talent and ninety-nine percent effort.' It takes more effort to climb the winding stairs than to ride an elevator. This isn't to say you shouldn't find ways to be efficient. But realise that building something worthwhile takes time and dedicated effort. It took King Solomon seven years to build the Temple! Literally? No! It doesn't take seven years for more than 200,000 men to construct a building that was not much larger than a tennis court! The seven years building is an allegory to the seven nerve centres, or chakras, through which your energy rises. It starts at your lowest chakra, or Root Chakra, at the base of the spine and eventually reaches the Crown Chakra at the top of the head. This rising energy is symbolic of a journey from your base/animal nature to your highest self – a journey which takes no short cuts.

No overnight success stories

But what about the overnight success stories I always hear about in the media?

The key word in this question is 'media'. The supposedly 'overnight' success of sportsmen, artists or entrepreneurs are media creations made to sound like quick accomplishments. But let me tell you, none are. As acclaimed author Sandra Cisneros once stated: 'One press account said I was an overnight success. I thought that was the longest night I've ever spent.' And comic actor Kevin Hart laid it straight when he said: 'Hollywood has a way of making everything seem like an overnight success.'

In reality, nobody achieves success overnight. Things that look like a quick ascension to great achievement typically are not.

Elvis Presley was fired by the Grand Ole Oprey after one performance and told he had no talent and would never amount to anything.

Henry Ford went broke five times before he founded the Ford Motor Company.

Harland Sanders' secret recipe for fried chicken was rejected one-thousand-and-nine times before acceptance.

Jim Carrey was booed off stage during his first comic stand-up in Toronto and failed his first audition for Saturday Night Live.

JK Rowling's *Harry Potter* script was rejected by twelve major publishers.

Katy Perry's first album sold only 200 copies and put the record company out of business.

Oprah Winfrey was fired from her first TV job because the producer thought she was unfit for television.

Stephen King's first novel was rejected 30 times.

Thomas Edison's teachers told him he was 'too stupid to learn anything'. He was also fired from his first two jobs for not being productive enough. In perhaps the ultimate story of climbing a symbolic winding staircase, Edison failed over 10,000 times before he finally invented the electric light bulb and changed the course of history. He couldn't see the top of the staircase for a long time, but he never gave up. Edison had faith in himself and a willingness to put in the hard work without taking shortcuts to get to where he wanted to go.

Challenges prepare average people for above-average success. You can't achieve your greatest dreams without an investment in mind, body and spirit. More won't come from doing less.

– 18 –
Manage your time effectively

Time management is big business. Corporations employ time management specialists to instruct employees how to schedule their days and complete their tasks on time. Life coaches assist individuals in learning how to juggle and balance time spent at work, with family and at leisure. Freemasonry has a method of time management that existed long before time management became a 'thing'. It's a working tool called a 24-inch gauge and through its use, Freemasons have been managing their time effectively for centuries.

Time management is a skill. It is the ability to plan and control how each hour of your day is spent to accomplish the highest efficiency in reaching your goals. Corporate buzz phrases such as 'setting goals', 'prioritising tasks', 'monitoring efficiency' and 'setting deadlines', all relate to time management. Many companies, especially in the finance and media sections, live and die by how well their executives and their employees manage time.

Time management is as old as time

Time management may seem like a concept that has taken corporate root over the last twenty years, but in actuality, time management is as old as time itself. Even the Bible offers plenty of verses about effectively managing one's time.

When you really begin pondering time and how much of it there is to work with, you will arrive at a simple truth: you can't change time, so you need to learn how to make the most of the time you have. It doesn't matter if you're the pope, the president, a pop star or a plumber, each of us has 168 hours in a week, and twenty-four hours in a day. Time is a level playing field for everyone. It does not discriminate. What sets a successful person apart is efficient use of time.

The 24-inch gauge
The first working tool given to a newly made Freemason is a 24-inch

gauge. As soon as one becomes an Entered Apprentice, he's handed this operative working tool for the symbolic instruction of managing time. That the founders of Freemasonry considered time management so important as to delegate the first working tool to its subject speaks volumes for the forward thinking of these wise men. They knew, as we do now, that the highest achievers all have one thing in common – they manage their time exceptionally well. They also knew that before any work is performed, the worker must determine how to divide his time effectively between the tasks at hand.

Freemasonry is an allegory for life, and life is work. A Freemason constantly works on self-improvement, but not in a selfish way. He does not undertake a one-eyed dedication to self-improvement at the neglect of time spent with friends and family. Says the Book of Ecclesiastes, which teaches lessons from the life of King Solomon: 'There is a time for everything, and a season for every activity under the heavens.' Simply put, if you want to get stuff done – all of it – find a way to manage your time and make it happen.

Like all the working tools in Freemasonry, the 24-inch gauge has an operative and speculative application. In the hands of a builder, the 24-inch gauge is used to measure stones for their placement into a structure. For the speculative Freemason, the 24-inch gauge is used to measure time, each inch of the gauge equating to one hour of a day.

A 24-inch gauge is a tool consisting of three equal parts divided into eight inches per part. Symbolically it teaches us to break the day into three equal parts measuring eight hours each: eight hours for the service of God and a distressed worthy brother; eight hours for work; and eight hours for refreshment and sleep.

Sounds a little crazy, doesn't it? Eight hours to the service of God? Eight hours for refreshment? How is that possible?

Your average day may consist of getting the kids ready for school, dropping them off, going to work, making deadlines, having a twenty-minute lunch break, attending after work drinks, helping the kids with their homework, spending time with your partner, catching up on your favourite TV show, walking the treadmill for twenty minutes, showering, checking social media and finally hitting the sack. The founders of Freemasonry could not possibly have considered all these aspects to a busy person's day when they designated the 24-inch gauge as a working tool for a lesson in time management!

A precious commodity

What's important here is the lesson, not a strict adherence to the eight-hour divisions. The 24-inch gauge teaches the value of time as a precious commodity that should not be spent lightly nor squandered. Before you can achieve anything in your day you must learn how to use your time effectively with measure and order. As Spanish philosopher, Baltasar Gracian said: 'All that really belongs to us is time; even he who has nothing else has that.'

The body's clock

Humans operate by two clocks. One sits on the wall and tells us the time. The other is your body clock; otherwise known as your biological clock. This internal clock doesn't run on batteries. But like a wall clock it is adjustable, not by a switch or a dial, but by circadian rhythm.

We do not operate in a 24-hour day by chance. Our bodies are set to a 24-hour cycle that regulates sleep, wakefulness and many other physiological processes. The biological clocks that control circadian rhythms are groupings of interacting molecules in cells throughout the body. A 'master clock' in the brain coordinates all the body clocks to be in synch.[56]

This internal clock is integral to your well-being. The incorrect setting of your internal clock throws off your circadian rhythm, which results in a negative impact on your body and its ability to function. Abnormal circadian rhythms, affected by external or environmental cues known as 'zeitbergers', can lead to serious health risks including cancer and cardiovascular disease. Abnormal circadian rhythms have also been associated with obesity, diabetes, depression, bipolar disorder, and seasonal affective disorder.[57]

Your body clock is located in the in the suprachiasmatic nucleus or nuclei (SCN) in the hypothalamus region of the brain above the optic chiasm.[58] The two hemispheres of the brain contain one suprachiasmatic nucleus each. This nucleus is a gathering of thousands of neurons which are the body's timekeepers. They set the clock on your glucose and insulin levels, sleeping patterns, feeding patterns, alertness, hormone production, brain wave activity, urine production and cell regeneration.[59]

The suprachiasmatic nuclei also control the production of melatonin, a hormone that makes you sleep. When natural light diminishes at sunset, the suprachiasmatic nuclei tell the pineal gland to develop more melatonin to induce drowsiness.

Did the developers of the speculative 24-inch gauge know about suprachiasmatic nuclei and optic chasms? Perhaps not. But they knew a very basic fact: without time allocated to your body's needs – without routine – your physical self deteriorates. And without a solid physical base, it's impossible to elevate your psychical self. A house without proper foundation – even one not made with hands – cannot stand.

Time is an individual experience

Steve Jobs once said: 'My favourite things in life don't cost any money. It's really clear that the most precious resource we all have is time.'

Time is a constantly diminishing commodity. Never take it for granted. Every morning you are handed 24 hours. They are one of the few things in this world that you get free of charge. If you had all the money in the world, you couldn't buy an extra hour. Time is a priceless treasure. It is also a treasure only you can experience.

Nobody else can live your time for you. Sure, others exist within your time frame, but they each exist on their own plane of time. You can make time to place your timeline alongside someone else's – helping your child with their homework, for example – but you can never experience their time for them nor change or alter their time plane.

Your time only exists now. What is past can never be repeated or altered. The future is never experienced, because the only experience one has is now. The only moment you can affect is the present. When you accept this fact, and work on using your present effectively, you will achieve a better use of time. If you worry about what might be, and wonder what might have been, you will ignore what is. As Buddha said: 'The secret of health for both mind and body is not to mourn for the past, worry about the future, but to live in the present moment wisely and earnestly.' In other words, practice mindfulness. Be aware of your actions, all of them, in this moment.

Freemasons have been practicing mindfulness in their lodge rooms for centuries. They close themselves to the outside world; forbid discussion of religion or politics so as to not detract from the harmony of the lodge. They choose to live their lodge experience in the present, focused on the tasks at hand, allowing their individual time frames to run alongside the time frames of their Brothers, so that a type of oneness is experienced. As many individuals sharing an experience, they realise that life unfolds in the present, and it is in the present that they must make the greatest use of time.

As author CS Lewis wrote: 'The future is something which everyone reaches at the rate of sixty minutes an hour, whatever he does, whoever he is.'

– 19 –
Avoid suspicion

Elvis Presley wasn't a Freemason, but he sung of a Masonic way of thinking when he warned about suspicious minds.

Freemasonry delivers a powerful exhortation to avoid suspicion. Suspicion is a product of paranoia, and people who experience paranoia think the world is trying to harm them, even though there is no evidence to support such behaviour.

Each degree in Freemasonry contains a specific charge designed to make a great impression on the individual. Charges communicate a responsibility or duty, as a command or specific lesson, providing earnest, solemn and authoritative instruction. Avoiding suspicion is a lesson in the second degree charge.

The first comprehensive compilation of Masonic charges was published by Dr James Anderson as a part of his *Constitutions* in 1723. In 1772, William Preston interpreted and embellished these charges and printed them in his book *Illustrations of Masonry*. In most American Grand Lodges, a brother appointed for the purpose delivers the Charge of the degree upon the brother newly initiated, passed, or raised. In most Grand Lodges these are Thomas Smith Webb's abbreviations of the original Prestonian Charges mentioned above.

Suspicion and the Upas tree
The second degree charge likens suspicion to an Upas tree, which we are told blights all healthy life and makes a desert round it.

The Upas is another name for the notoriously poisonous *Antiaris Toxicaria* tree. The latex of *Antiaris Toxicaria* contains intensely toxic cardenolides (a type of steroid) and was traditionally used as a poison for Indonesian arrows and darts. In China, the tree is known as the 'Poison Arrow Tree'. Upas is said to be so deadly that, according to legend, one cannot reach the trunk of the tree before falling down dead. An account of the tree's toxicity published in *The London Magazine* in 1783, claims that the poison from an Upas tree destroys all animal life in a 15 mile or more radius.

Just as nothing can live at the base of an Upas tree, so Freemasonry tells us nothing fair and pure (beautiful and good) thrives in the shadow of suspicion.

The charge to the Fellowcraft to avoid suspicion is two-pronged. He must avoid suspicion of others and avoid developing any suspicion about himself. Steer clear of any behaviour that may cause others to become suspicious of your actions. Once the dye of suspicion is cast, it is difficult to clean. As Gandhi said: 'Suspicion is not less an enemy to virtue than to happiness; he that is already corrupt is naturally suspicious, and he that becomes suspicious will quickly be corrupt.'

Take off your hyper-vigilant glasses

British poet Ben Johnson wrote of suspicion: '...it may well be called poor mortals plague for, like a pestilence, it doth infect the houses of the brain till not a thought, or motion, in the mind, be free from the black poison of suspect'.

The suspicious mind is always ill-at-ease with those around it. A suspicious person looks for hidden meanings in things people say and do. They hunt for hidden agendas in the actions of others, which aren't hidden at all because, in reality, such ulterior motives don't exist.

What an exhausting way to live! Constantly viewing the world through hyper-vigilant glasses is a one-way road to a paranoid personality disorder in which your mind operates in a constant state of edginess. Instead of investing precious mental energies in worthwhile projects, the suspicious mind, left unchecked, blows its wad on twisting what is clear cut into a blur of over analysis. This over analysis leads to paralysis. While wasting time dissecting every word, action and reaction, the suspicious mind doesn't realise that everyone else is getting on with their lives.

Freemasonry teaches 'no path so straight but to suspicion's eye looks torturous and bent from its true end'. Simply put, when you begin viewing the world through suspicion goggles, everything looks bent. The more distrustful and suspicious the world becomes, the more twisted your path through it.

Avoid suspicion. This is a key charge in Freemasonry. Avoid creating something out of nothing. Don't read too much into situations in which there is nothing to read. If someone is running late for a meeting with you, don't fuel your mind with suspicious reasons as to why. There's no ulterior motive for their lateness. They're not plotting against you or deliberately arriving late to grind on your nerves. Don't colour something grey that is black and white. Sometimes, people are just late. And when that person finally arrives at the meeting, don't sit across from them with suspicion on your mind. Don't create wild scenarios in your head. Avoid paranoia by simply asking them why they were late. You'll most likely receive an answer so simple and boring that you'll feel silly for having asked at all. *I caught every stop light. I got a flat tire. I stopped for gas. I overslept my alarm.*

Don't become as the fabled Upas and blight all healthy life around you. Release yourself from the feeling that everyone is out to hurt you. It's not the case. The world is full of genuine people who deserve a chance to not be seen through suspicion goggles. When you're suspicious, you pass judgement and more often than not do so without being armed with all the facts. Don't believe me?

A question of judgement
You see a man with dark eyes, dark hair, tanned skin and a thick, dark beard. Your cultural conditioning and built in fears – your suspicion goggles – view him as a terrorist. He's an immoral human being out to do injury to yourself and others. He speaks a foreign language and he's constantly reading his holy book. Perhaps, you think, he's strapped with bombs and ready to press the button that will send him to paradise and his 72 virgins.

Do you know who the man really is? Of course you don't. You're passing judgement without the facts. You're letting paranoia and suspicion form a picture in your mind of who this man is.

The man is married. He has a beautiful wife, Effie, and two young daughters, Stefanie and Mary. This man you labeled a terrorist does a lot of work in the local community, gives his time to help charitable organisations, and attends church three times a week. He is a source of great comfort and joy for many people, especially the elderly who knock on his door, bring him cakes and biscuits, and feel better about themselves after a visit with him. His daughters are top students in their classes. His wife works as a travel agent, and he enjoys reading, watching soccer and good wine.

The man is not a terrorist. He is a Greek Orthodox priest. His name is Father Dimitri. Of course, you will never know this because you only see Father Dimitri through suspicion goggles that project your own unresolved fears.

What's the lesson?

If you don't know something about others or a situation, avoid turning a hypothesis or coincidences into a state of facts in your mind.

A lesson from George Washington

When George Washington was 16 years old, he wrote a paper entitled '110 Rules of Civility and Decent Behaviour in Company and Conversation'. The rules were based on a set originally composed by French Jesuits in 1595 and played a large role in shaping Washington into the man and leader he became. So profoundly good was the character of George Washington that in 1814 Thomas Jefferson wrote about the first American president: '...on the whole, his character was, in its mass perfect, in nothing bad, in few points indifferent; and it may truly be said that never did nature and fortune combine more perfectly to make a man great'.

One of Washington's rules of civility states: 'Be not apt to relate news if you know not the truth thereof.'

Suspicious people are so caught up in the news of their own bent beliefs that they cannot possibly see the truth about a person or a scenario. The above example about the Greek Orthodox priest, whom through suspicion goggles was seen to be a terrorist, aptly relays the dangers of being too caught in the news of one's own (false) beliefs to see the truth. Washington is telling you to always confirm your sources. In the example of the Greek Orthodox priest, the source of information was the suspicious person's built-in fears and prejudices.

Hold on, you may be thinking. *Isn't it sometimes better to be safe than sorry? The priest could well have been a terrorist, right? Then I would not be wrong to have viewed him through suspicion goggles.*

The duality of things

To pass judgement on Father Dimitri without having confirmed your sources is an act of suspicion, which is the negative end of the pole of skepticism. Given that everything in life is duality, and duality is the opposite poles of the same thing, what then is the positive end of this pole? Investigation.

One who investigates (positive pole) asks, 'What is the evidence?'

One who is suspicious (negative pole) does not even consider the evidence.

Investigation is healthy. Freemasonry doesn't warn against skepticism. In fact, it encourages skeptic investigation. Investigative skeptics search for facts and extract the laws of nature. Unlike the suspicious skeptic, the investigative skeptic assumes nothing and checks everything. At the other end of this pole, suspicious skeptics invent their own facts and stick to them. Anything not understood is regarded as harmful. A suspicious person takes nothing at face value. They consider the world as nonsensical and chaotic. Everyone is constantly conspiring against the suspicious skeptic.

Suspicious skepticism may be expressed as hostility in an aggressive person, and as nihilism in a passive person. Either way, a suspicious person tends to be avoided. As such, much of the world's beauty passes them by.

Doubt breeds suspicion

Suspicion begins with doubt. Doubt breeds suspicion, which in turn breeds anxiety. Anxiety leads to fear, and fear breeds self-protection. Self-protection leads to withdrawal, which leads to loneliness and the blasting of self-worth. Bad habits are formed, including addictive behaviours, which further compound the problems mentioned above. Sadly, however, the suspicious person rarely suspects that they themselves are the main cause of their misery

'Suspicion is the companion of mean souls', wrote Thomas Paine, 'and the bane of all good society'.

As an investigative skeptic armed with the information presented here, it's little wonder Freemasonry places such great importance on admonishing its members to: 'Avoid suspicion; for like the fabled Upas it blights all healthy life and makes a desert round it. Nothing so fair, nothing so pure can live but by suspicion may be marred and blasted. No path so straight but to suspicion's eye looks torturous and bent from its true end.'

– 20 –
The Golden Rule

In 2005, a British television network surveyed more than 40,000 people and asked them to create their own version of the Ten Commandments. The most popular commandment from those surveyed was the Golden Rule: 'Treat others as you want to be treated.' This moral rule, encompassing the Three Great Tenets of Freemasonry – Brotherly Love, Relief and Truth – has been lauded and preached by successful Freemasons for centuries.

In 1763, French Freemason, writer and philosopher Voltaire, said: 'The single fundamental and immutable law for men is the following: Treat others as you would be treated. This law is from nature itself: it cannot be torn from the heart of man.'

In 1902, Freemason businessman JC Penney opened the Golden Rule Store. He believed in treating his customers how he wanted to be treated. Forty-eight years later he published a book entitled, *Fifty Years with the Golden Rule.*

President Theodore Roosevelt, a Freemason, said in the first *Boy Scout Handbook*: 'No man is a good citizen unless he so acts as to show that he actually uses the Ten Commandments and translates the golden rule into his life conduct.'

Reverend Joseph Fort Newton writes at the conclusion of the outstanding Masonic book *The Builders*: 'High above all dogmas that divide, all bigotries that blind, will be written the simple words of the one eternal religion – the Fatherhood of God, the brotherhood of man, the moral law, the golden rule, and the hope of a life everlasting!'

Brotherly Love is the first of the Three Great Tenets of Freemasonry, and there can be no better display of Brotherly Love to your fellow human being than to do unto him as you would want done to yourself. It's little wonder, therefore, that several Masonic Lodges around the world are named Golden Rule Lodge, including: Ann Arbor, Michigan (USA); San Jose, California (USA); Knightstown, Indiana (USA); Wakefield,

Massachusetts; Oakleigh, Victoria (Australia); Pense, Saskatchewan (Canada); Estrie, Quebec (Canada); London (England).

The most well-known version of the Golden Rule is that espoused by Jesus: 'Do unto others as you would have them do unto you.' However, Jesus was not the first teacher to preach this moral lesson. Jesus tells us this when he says, 'This is the law of the prophets', stating clearly that the Golden Rule was taught by those who came before him.

The ethic of reciprocity

For as long as men have instructed in ethics, the ethic of reciprocity has existed. A version of the Golden Rule exists in every great teaching system and can be found in at least 18 religions. Confucius phrased it perfectly 500 years before Christ when he said: 'Never impose on others what you would not choose for yourself.'

Ancient Egyptian concept of Maat dates to as early as 2000 BCE. It states: 'Now this is the command: Do to the doer to cause that he do thus to you.'

The Hindu rule of Dharma states: 'One should never do that to another which one regards as injurious to one's own self.'

Islam preaches: 'No one of you is a believer until he loves for his brother what he loves for himself.'

In the Baha'i Faith it is written: 'Ascribe not to any soul that which thou wouldst not have ascribed to thee, and say not that which thou doest not.'

Zoroastrianism teaches: 'That nature alone is good which refrains from doing unto another whatsoever is not good for itself.'

Jainism specifies: 'A man should wander about treating all creatures as he himself would be treated.'

Buddhism teaches: 'Treat not others in ways that you yourself would find hurtful.'

Wrote Plato (428-348 BCE), in his dialogue *Crito:* 'One should never do wrong in return, nor mistreat any man, no matter how one has been mistreated by him.'

When Hilel (110 BC-10 CE) was asked for a summary of the teachings of the entire Torah, he answered: 'That which is hateful to you, do not do to your fellow. That is the whole Torah; the rest is the explanation; go and learn it.'[60]

A moral axiom

Freemasons aspire to follow the Golden Rule, the appeal of which comes from its simplicity. It is the philosophical and moral equivalent of a mathematical axiom.

What is an axiom?

It's something that is so evident or well-established that it is accepted without question. A mathematical axiom, for example, is: if a = b then b = a. Numbers are symmetric around the equals sign. As Euclid said: 'Things equal to the same thing are equal to each other.' The word axiom derives from the Greek axioma, meaning something thought of as worthy or fit, which is true for the Golden Rule.

Successful business interactions, from the smallest basement office to boardrooms of the largest companies on Earth, rely on the idea of the Golden Rule. Don't screw over someone else's business unless you want your own business screwed over. Success in business is also dependent on listening. The Golden Rule is a two-way street: if you want someone to listen to you, you must listen to them.

Good managers enact the Golden Rule in dealing with employees. A tyrannical manager does not gain the respect of his workers. But a manager who puts himself in the employee's shoes, extending him the same respect he himself demands, gets the very best out of those in his employ.

Dale Carnegie's Teaching

In October 1936, Dale Carnegie published a self-help book that would go on to sell tens of millions of copies. *How to Win Friends and Influence People* is still as relevant today as it was when first released. Its aim is to get readers out of a mental rut, give them new thoughts, new visions and new ambitions. If you want to make friends quicker and easier; increase your popularity; win people to your way of thinking; sign new clients; increase earning power; and keep your human contacts smooth and pleasant, this is the book for you. And do you know what is at the crux of this riotously popular and time-honoured book? The Golden Rule.

Writes Carnegie:

> *Philosophers have been speculating on the rules of human relationships for thousands of years, and there has evolved only one important precept. Zoroaster taught it to his followers in Persia twenty-five hundred years ago. Confucius preached it in China. Lao-Tse, the founder of Taoism, taught it to his disciples. Buddha preached it on the banks of the Ganges. The sacred books of Hinduism taught it a thousand years before that. Jesus summed it up in one thought – probably the most*

important rule in the world: 'Do unto others as you would have others do unto you.' You want a feeling that you are important in your little world. You don't want to listen to cheap, insincere flattery, but you do crave sincere appreciation. All of us want that. So let's obey the golden rule, and give unto others what we would have others give unto us.

Two particular rules in George Washington's '110 Rules of Civility and Decent Behaviour', inculcate the idea behind the Golden Rule. Washington's very first rule states: 'Every Action done in Company, ought to be with Some Sign of Respect, to those that are Present.' Simply put: respect one another.

Washington's sixth rule more greatly alludes to the Golden Rule: 'Sleep not when others Speak, Sit not when others stand, Speak not when you Should hold your Peace, walk not on when others Stop.' In layman's terms: Don't do something you don't want someone doing to you. You wouldn't like it if someone walked ahead of you while you stopped to tie a shoelace. You wouldn't like it if someone was off in a daydream while you were talking to them. You wouldn't like it if someone chimed into your conversation when it was none of their business. Don't do these things to anyone else.

Give brotherly love, relief and truth in all your words and actions. Be civil. Be human. Adhere to the Golden Rule and see how much happier your life becomes, and the lives of those around you.

− 21 −
My name is Caution

In the Entered Apprentice degree, the newly made Freemason is symbolically given a new name: Caution. He is admonished to be cautious over all his words and actions, especially on the subject of Freemasonry in the presence of its enemies.

Should a newly made Freemason be careful not to spill the beans on Freemasonry's teachings when he's around conspiracy nuts? Is this what the admonition means? Not really.

Analysis of Masonic instruction is a form of code cracking. You can't take the words at face value. The new Entered Apprentice just took a solemn obligation not to talk about any of the secrets of Freemasonry, so why would he need to be pulled aside and told to watch what he says around anti-Masons? It makes no sense.

However, when you study the instruction from an allegorical point of view – remembering that Freemasonry is a system of teaching veiled in allegory – the admonition to be cautious is a vital lesson on the promotion of happiness and well-being.

Freemasonry is about self-improvement. When you understand this, you have a skeleton key to unlock many of the organisation's teachings. Substitute the words 'Freemasonry' and 'lodge' with 'yourself' and you will make greater sense of the lessons being taught. Let's do this with the lesson of caution given to the newly made Entered Apprentice: *You are given a new name, Caution, which is to teach you to be cautious over all your words and actions, especially on the subject of yourself, when in the presence of your enemies.*

Makes a little more sense now, right? But what about the word 'enemies'? Who are these enemies around whom we must exercise caution?

Enemies at your gate

The enemies in question are not other people talking bad about Freemasonry. They are those things that do the greatest damage to yourself and, therefore, are your enemies. They are the same enemies at the door of your personal lodge protected by your personal Tyler. The true enemies are your negative thoughts and actions, more easily summarised as your negative vibrations.

Albert Einstein said: 'Everything in life is a vibration.' We are putting out and receiving positive and negative vibes all the time. Our bodies are in a constant state of vibration; indeed, they are vibration as a group of atoms in a constant state of motion. Everything we see, everything we hear, everything we think, is vibration. Everything that manifests in your life is matching the vibrations of your thoughts.[61] Nature vibrates at different frequencies. Therefore, the frequency of your thoughts can and does affect the frequency of your body. This is why you can think yourself ill and manifest that illness physically. It's all vibrational! As the Buddha said: 'Sabbe Dhamma vedana samosarana – anything that arises in the mind starts flowing as a sensation on the body. We are the same as plants, as trees, as other people, as the rain that falls. We consist of that which is around us, we are the same as everything.'

The Principle of Vibration, as detailed in *The Kybalion*, states:

> *Nothing rests; everything moves; everything vibrates. This Principle explains that the differences between different manifestations of Matter, Energy, Mind, and even Spirit, result largely from varying rates of Vibration. From THE ALL, which is Pure Spirit, down to the grossest form of Matter, all is in vibration – the higher the vibration, the higher the position in the scale. The vibration of Spirit is at such an infinite rate of intensity and rapidity that it is practically at rest – just as a rapidly moving wheel seems to be motionless. And at the other end of the scale, there are gross forms of matter whose vibrations are so low as to seem at rest. Between these poles, there are millions upon millions of varying degrees of vibration. From corpuscle and electron, atom and molecule, to worlds and universes, everything is in vibratory motion. This is also true on the planes of energy and force (which are but varying degrees of vibration); and also on the mental planes (whose states depend upon vibrations); and even on to the spiritual planes.*

According to the unknown authors of *The Kybalion:* 'He who understands the Principle of Vibration, has grasped the sceptre of Power.'

Our vibes are powerful stuff, and anything powerful should be wielded with caution.

Thought is everywhere

Nothing exists without thought. You're reading this book because you thought to do so. You're wearing clothes because you thought to get dressed. You work because you thought to undertake employment. Cars, planes, trams, trains, buses, boats and all other forms of transportation only exist because someone thought to invent them. War is the result of thought. Medicine is the result of thought. Space exploration is the result of thought. The thoughts of what foods you eat directly impact the health of your body. The thoughts of what exercise you undertake (or think to not undertake) directly impact the shape of your body. Someone else's happiness or sorrow may be the result of your thoughts. You exist because your parents thought to partake in the act of intercourse that lead to your conception. It is through thought that all is possible.

Thoughts are everywhere; everything is thought, and thought is vibration.

All we do in life begins with thought. Your conscious mind plays your thoughts over and over and these are embedded on your subconscious mind. These thoughts are powerful vibrations, which in turn attract similar vibrations into your life. If you're feeling disillusioned or upset, you're resonating unhappy vibrations and thus attracting unhappiness into your life. Feelings are conscious awareness of your vibrations. You may feel helplessly shackled to these feelings but remember, your thoughts are your choice, and therefore you and you alone are choosing to resonate a frequency of unhappiness. Only you have the power to change the vibrations of your thoughts from negative to positive.

The cautious seldom err

Confucius said, 'The cautious seldom err'. He's right. If you're cautious over your thoughts and actions, it's difficult to end up on the wrong side of life's tracks. This is the true meaning of the Entered Apprentice's lesson to be cautious around the enemies of Freemasonry. These enemies are not Freemasonry's detractors. The true enemy we all face is our way of thinking, which in turn produces our actions.

Freemasons exercise caution over their words and actions, which are results of thoughts. Be cautious of what you think because those thoughts could end up as words, and words carry tremendous power.

Words are the product of thought and can also affect the way we think. Sounds a little mind-bending? Let me explain further.

Words cannot change physical reality. I can't say, 'Wall, fall down' and the wall falls down. However, words can affect the way we perceive the world around us. The wall won't fall down when I tell it to, but if I tell myself, 'I can climb that wall, it is not that high, I'm fit, I'm confident, and I have the necessary tools to do so,' chances are I will climb it. However, if I tell myself, 'That wall is too high! I'm too heavy to climb it, I don't know how to climb it, I don't have any rope, I'm scared of heights. It's too hard!', chances are I will not climb it.

Words carry energy and vibration, as does everything else in the world. The more you talk yourself down, the more you worry, the more you play the victim, and the more you criticise yourself, the more negative energy you attract. Negative talk is the result of negative thoughts, and negative thinking is the true enemy of yourself.

Be cautious of your thoughts. If you're a negative Nelly, recognise this thought process and change it! It won't be easy. For many people negative thinking is a habit, and habits are hard to break. But the good news is they can be broken! It won't happen overnight, but a change in mindset will happen.

Next time you catch yourself self-criticising, kick those negative thoughts to the curb and shift your perspective. Laugh at yourself and replace the negative mindset with a positive one. Start small. Exercise caution over one thought at a time. When you wake up in the morning, launch a pre-emptive strike against your enemies! Look at yourself in the mirror and say something positive. It may seem silly at first, but the more you do it, the more you will start to believe it. Eventually, you will develop a habit of defeating your mental enemies first thing in the morning and when you start to believe your positive thoughts, you will start attracting greater positivity into your life.

– 22 –
Riding the goat

There are aspects of Freemasonry that do not appear in any of the lectures or rituals yet are still familiar to every initiate. One of these is the often-made reference to 'riding the goat'. It is not uncommon for a candidate to be told before initiation that he must 'ride the goat.'

I've known candidates who became convinced that part of their initiation required them to ride an actual live goat around the lodge room! Let me assure you, riding a physical goat plays no part in Masonic teaching.

Considering, however, that Freemasonry is 'veiled in allegory' and that nothing in Freemasonry is random, we must assume that to 'ride the goat' is symbolic of something. But what exactly?

Giddy up goat!

There never has been, and never will be, a goat used in any form of Masonic initiation. If you ever find yourself in a lodge that employs the use of a live goat or a mock goat, leave immediately. Such a lodge is irregular and not participating in true Freemasonry.

You will, however, hear Freemasons talk about 'riding the goat'. It's not uncommon for a candidate to be asked if he is ready to ride the goat. Sadly, most Freemasons have little to no idea as to the symbolism behind the question they're asking.

When one asks if the candidate has ridden the goat or is prepared to do such, one is actually asking a very important question about the candidate's character. As you will see, if a candidate is not prepared to ride the goat, he is not qualified to become a Freemason.

Let's clear up some misconceptions and unveil the true symbolic meaning of 'riding the goat'.

No goats allowed

There is a belief that Masons actually ride goats as part of their 'secret and weird' rituals.

Why is this?

The answer is in part due to anti-Masonic propaganda. Take, for example, Wiccan witch High Priest William Schnoebellan, a former 32nd degree Mason of whom you'll find many videos on Youtube. Schnoebellan constantly launches tirades against the Masonic fraternity he was once a part of. In one of his rants, Schnoebellan says:

I was kept in an anteroom. The fellow who was in charge of keeping an eye on me said that I should not worry about riding the goat in the initiation – most guys did it and never fell off. Another fellow came in and said that I shouldn't believe any of 'those stories' about riding the goat. A third fellow winked at me and said they'd only lost a couple of candidates in the last year through death by violence, so I shouldn't worry. It was all done in the manner of good-natured teasing.

Schnoebellan then reveals the pagan origins of this blasphemous ceremony, stating:

In the many initiations I observed or actually took part in, I saw a lot of variations of this kind of fraternity house humour. The only common thing in the many jokes and disturbing allusions was this business about riding the goat. That is interesting when one recalls Albert Pike's teaching about the he-goat of the witches' sabbath, and the way witches in the Middle Ages demonstrated their allegiance to Satan. They had to consent to sexual intercourse with the goat.

A high priest would rig up a goat's head and demand followers perform the so-called *osculum infamum* (obscene kiss) on the goat's backside to show their fealty to Satan. Pagan imagery painted the mischievous god Pan as resembling the appearance of a goat with hoofed feet.

Witches in the Middle Ages were said to have participated in orgies in which Satan appeared riding a goat. Witches performed fearfully blasphemous ceremonies of 'raising the devil' and initiation into Satanic rites. As Masonic ritual practices its own (symbolic) 'raising' from the dead, so the public mind wrongly transferred the witchcraft beliefs – including riding the goat – to Freemasonry.

Hollywood also had its role in the belief that Freemasons ride real goats. The embryonic film industry of the early 1900s sought to capitalise on the popularity of fraternal societies by using fraternal goats, mainly for comedic purposes.

Animator Earl Hurd used a goat in the 1916 film *Bobby Bumps Starts a Lodge,* released through Paramount Pictures.

The 1927 comedy short, *Should a Mason Tell?* centres on the lies a husband tells his wife about his initiation into a Masonic lodge, of which a goat plays a prominent role.

The shape of a goat's head also contributed to the goat's standing as a Satanic beast. The horns, ears and long chin of a goat resemble an inverted five-pointed star, or inverted pentagram. In some forms of Wicca (witchcraft), an inverted pentagram is the symbol of the third and highest degree. Also known as the Sigil of Baphomet, the inverted pentagram with the head of a goat at its centre is the copyrighted logo of the Church of Satan.

French master occultist of the 16th century, Eliphas Levi, wrote:

The Pentagram, with two horns in the ascendant, represents Satan, or the goat of the Sabbath, and with the single horn in the ascendant it is the sign of the Saviour. It is the figure of the human body with the four members and a point representing the head; a human figure-head downward naturally represents the demon, that is, intellectual subversion, disorder, and folly.

Manly P. Hall wrote in *The Secret Teachings of All Ages*:

The pentagram is used extensively in black magic, but when so used its form always differs in one of three ways: The star may be broken at one point by not permitting the converging lines to touch; it may be inverted by having one point down and two up; or it may be distorted by having the points of varying lengths. When used in black magic, the pentagram is called the "sign of the cloven hoof," or the footprint of the Devil. The star with two points upward is also called the "Goat of Mendes" because the inverted star is the same shape as a goat's head. When the upright star turns and the upper point falls to the bottom, it signifies the fall of the Morning Star.

Give up the goat

Why are Freemasons really said to 'ride the goat'?

Riding the goat is associated with Masonic initiation. Coming from the world of darkness, the (Cowan) candidate for the Entered Apprentice degree is tested for his worthiness to join Freemasonry.

To be admitted into Freemasonry, one must leave behind his ego, lusts, and material desires, all of which are symbolised by a goat's head, or inverted pentagram.

How?

A regular pentagram with one point up represents intelligence (up point) ruling the dominating instincts of the flesh (four points beneath). When inverted, however, the five-pointed star signifies man standing on his head. His body is above his brain. His reason is dominated by the lusts of the body, and as such he is in a state of chaos. The inverted pentagram looks like a goat's head, with its two horns and long chin pointed downwards. It is this representation that has come to symbolise the devil, representative of the lower aspects of our human nature. This is the goat of Freemasonry – our animal side. It is your base instincts; the lower vibrational self; your worst aspects.

Riding the goat, therefore, signifies dominance over the devil aspects of our nature – the animal instincts sublimated into spiritual assets.

When one rides an animal, one has dominance over that animal. To ride a goat shows symbolic domination over the animal of our lusts and desires. The goat does not ride the initiate, the initiate rides the goat. He has dominion over the animal, symbolically dominion over the material/base nature/animal part of himself.

To prove ready for initiation into higher learning, one must first exercise control over his animal self. One must ride the goat!

– 23 –
Understanding the real 47th Proposition of Euclid

The 47th Proposition of Euclid has long held a place of reverence in Freemasonry. The third degree lecture tells us: 'The Forty-seventh Problem of Euclid teaches Masons to be general lovers of the arts and sciences.'

That the lecture offers us no further information on the 47th Proposition of Euclid, what it is or how Freemasons should use it, raised a giant red flag the first time I heard it mentioned.

Why is this symbol, presented on various tracing boards and on the Past Master's jewel in many jurisdictions, only given one short sentence of mention? By Masonic standards, this single sentence is a weak one. Surely there are numerous symbols in the Craft that teach Masons to be general lovers of the arts and sciences? Why specifically mention the 47th Proposition of Euclid?

What is the 47th PROPOSITION of Euclid?
Anderson's Constitutions of 1723 calls the 47th Proposition of Euclid an 'amazing proposition'. But what's so amazing about it?

At the time of its discovery, not by Euclid but by Pythagoras, and earlier than he by the Egyptians, the revelation that in any right-angled triangle the longest side, or hypotenuse, equals when squared the combined squares of the two other sides would have indeed been amazing. But these days every high school student is taught that in a right-angled triangle the square of the hypotenuse is equal to the sum of the squares of the other two sides, known by the equation: $a^2+b^2=c^2$.

Surely this is no great lesson to a Freemason?

Yes, the 47th Proposition of Euclid has allowed man to do amazing things, such as reach into space and measure the distance of the stars; dig tunnels on opposite sides of a mountain that meet together exactly at the centre; navigate oceans and locate himself in the middle of the water with no land in sight; survey land, mark off boundaries, and construct nearly everything from churches to shopping malls. This information, again, learned in high school, is great for Operative Masons, but what possible

204 — FREEMASONRY'S HIDDEN BRAIN SCIENCE

reason is there for the mention of the 47th Proposition of Euclid in the lecture of the highest degree in Freemasonry?

The curious brevity of information pertaining to the 47th Proposition of Euclid warrants further investigation and begs the question: Of what purpose is reference to the 47th Proposition of Euclid to the *Speculative* Mason?

Let's speculate

There is absolutely no reason why the 47th Proposition of Euclid is given such note in the third degree lecture. Yes, it has allowed mankind to accomplish many great feats of engineering, but the ability to form a right angled triangle in which the hypotenuse is equal to the sum of the squares of the two other sides is useless to us as Freemasons seeking to raise our inner master, that is, to achieve higher consciousness and ignite our divine spark through transcending our lower nature by improving our moral worth.

If Freemasonry is Moral Science, the 47th Proposition of Euclid must – must! – present a philosophical lesson applicable to the interior work of self-improvement, not a mathematical lesson without any internal application.

Euclid

Euclid was a Greek mathematician who lived in Alexandria around 300 BCE. He is often referred to as the Father of Geometry and was author of one of the most important and successful mathematical textbooks of all time, *Elements*, which represents the culmination of a mathematical revolution that had taken place in Greece up to that time. Euclid's work included writings on the division of geometrical figures into parts in given ratios; the mathematical theory of mirrors and reflections; the determination of the location of objects in the celestial sphere; and texts on optics and music.

Elements is a lucid and comprehensive compilation and explanation of all the known mathematics of his time, including the work of Pythagoras, Hippocrates, Theudius, Theaetetus and Eudoxus. In all, it contains 465 theorems and proofs, described in a clear, logical and elegant style, and using only a compass and a straight edge.

Elements consists of thirteen books, the first of which outlines the fundamental propositions of plane geometry, including the three cases in which triangles are congruent, various theorems involving parallel lines, the theorem regarding the sum of the angles in a triangle, and the Pythagorean theorem.

Proposition XLVII (47) states: In right-angled triangles the square on the side opposite the right angle equals the sum of the squares on the sides containing the right angle.

The hunt for clues

Even after looking into the life and works of Euclid, we are no closer to an answer as to why the 47th Proposition is given mention in the third degree lecture for the Speculative Mason focused on interior work. We must remember, however, that Masonic ritual was written by men ahead of their time. They did not use newspaper directness, but rather concealed their lessons, hid them from the masses, making them available only to those willing to probe deep.

As we probe and look for clues and signposts as to what the ritual writers are trying to tell us, we should take into consideration the time period during which much of the ritual was written: The Age of Enlightenment.

The Age of Enlightenment

The Age of Enlightenment was a sprawling intellectual, philosophical, cultural, and social movement that spread through England, France, Germany, and other parts of Europe during the 1700s. The intellectual movement emphasised reason, individualism, and skepticism, and presented a challenge to traditional religious views. Its roots are usually traced to the foundation of the Royal Society in 1660, and 1680s England, where in a three-year period Isaac Newton published his *Principia Mathematica* (1686), and John Locke his *'Essay Concerning Human Understanding'* (1689), two works that provided the mathematical, scientific and philosophical base for the Enlightenment's major advances. The era's motto is perhaps best summed up in a quote from German philosopher Immanuel Kant who wrote, in his 1784 essay *'What is Enlightenment?'*: 'Dare to know! Have courage to use your own reason!'

Before this period, knowledge came from two sources: the Bible and the classics, such as Aristotle and Plato. Many thinkers, however, began to question authority following the encouragement of the questioning mind during the Renaissance. Man's ability to reason, think and evaluate became another source of authority, and people began the philosophical study of 'how we know what we know.' The Age of Enlightenment also replaced the pessimistic view of the world, in which all men were scripturally defined as sinners who would bring about the world's end, with an idea that man could reason, apply that reason and therefore change any problem. Sin was ignorance, and ignorance could be fixed with knowledge and education.

Out of this mode of thinking Freemasonry was born in its modern form. Freemasons were free thinkers, learned in a variety of subjects, and taught that man had a spiritual nature as well as a physical nature. Freemasonry taught morals, self-control, and how to reach for a higher standard in conducting one's life, without the dogma of religion. It was not an irreligious or anti-political group, but rather a gathering of the curious at a time when established rules of the church and state were not generally subject to challenge.

Some of the greatest philosophical minds of the Enlightenment Age were or had connections to Freemasonry, including Sir Francis Bacon (he may or may not have been a Freemason), John Locke (he was most likely a Freemason), Voltaire (a Freemason), and Sir Isaac Newton (very likely a Freemason). Newton's personal secretary was none other than John Theophilus Desaguliers, a French-born British natural philosopher, clergyman, engineer and Freemason who was elected to the Royal Society in 1714. Desaguliers became the Grand Master of the Premier Grand Lodge of England and helped James Anderson draw up the rules in the *Constitutions of the Freemasons* published in 1723. He was active in the establishment of Masonic charity, and initiated Francis, Duke of Lorraine (1708-65) into Freemasonry. Francis, who later become Holy Roman Emperor, also presided when Frederick, Prince of Wales, became a Freemason in 1731.

Not the Euclid you're looking for

Among the many prominent philosophers of the Age of Enlightenment, the signposts and clues to solving the riddle of the inclusion of the 47th Proposition of Euclid in Masonic ritual point us in the direction of a Dutch Jewish philosopher of Portuguese descent named Benedict Spinoza, who was not a Freemason but has, I believe, made great impact on our ritual.

Born in 1632, Spinoza compiled his greatest works during a time in the Age of Enlightenment when Freemasonry was evolving rapidly into its modern form.

The Church councils and synods of Holland took energetic measures against Spinoza's work, which appeared anonymously in 1670. Up to 1676 at least thirty-seven decisions or edicts against the work had appeared. Both loved and loathed during his time, Spinoza was issued the harshest writ of *herem* (a ban or ostracism) ever pronounced upon a member of the Portuguese-Jewish community in Amsterdam, and his books were put on the Catholic Church's Index of Forbidden Books.

Spinoza, who worked all his life as a humble glass grinder, turning down many rewards, honours, and prestigious teaching positions, is revered in modern philosophical circles. When Albert Einstein was asked if he believed in God, the scientist replied: 'I believe in Spinoza's God who reveals himself in the orderly harmony of what exists, not in a God who concerns himself with fates and actions of human beings.'

Spinoza encouraged freedom of thought, democracy, intellectual knowledge of God, and love for one's neighbour, which sounds very similar to the lessons of Freemasonry.

He believed that the true Word of God was to act justly, give charity and love one's neighbour, and he was disgusted that different religious groups were fighting each other over small discrepancies in how to interpret the Bible texts. He rejected the belief that the Jewish people are "chosen," and therefore superior to others, that prophets received revelation in a supernatural way, or that miracles were anything more than natural events that had been misunderstood.

Spinoza was considered by Friedrich Hegel as the greatest philosopher ever, and his magnum opus was a book (published posthumously) entitled *Ethics*.

Spinoza was greatly influenced by Descartes, who considered geometry to be an ideal example of man's ability to use his reason in order to arrive at certain truth. Ancient Greek philosopher Plato also had great respect for geometry. On the front of Plato's Academy in ancient Greece was written, 'Let no one ignorant of geometry enter here'.

Spinoza chose to write *Ethics* as if it were an actual geometric proof. He used axioms (e.g.: 'Everything which exists, exists either in itself or in something else') and definitions (e.g.: 'By substance, I mean that which is in itself, and is conceived through itself') to come up with propositions, proofs, and corollaries in order to demonstrate with geometric certainty to others his beliefs about God and the world.

X Marks the Spot!

Here is where things get really interesting. Spinoza wrote *Ethics* in the same fashion as Euclid wrote *Elements*, that is in the style of mathematical proofs, thus establishing Spinoza as the Euclid of the Age of Enlightenment!

The Masonic ritual writers would have been well versed in Spinoza's Euclidean-styled *Ethics*, which Richard A. Graeter 33° describes as thus: 'Ethics is a book that begins with God and ends with human freedom. At first, Ethics seems to be an inscrutable chain of obtuse propositions, but closer examination proves it to be a journey whereby the mind embarks on an exodus from a state of bondage to false beliefs and systems of power to the promised land of clarity and self-knowledge.'[62]

We find our final clue — our X-marks-the-spot moment — in the culmination of Spinoza's writings: his 47th Proposition.

Prop. XLVII. The human mind has an adequate knowledge of the eternal and infinite essence of God.

This is the answer we have searched for!

The Masonic ritual writers in using the 47th Proposition of Euclid in the third degree lecture were not pointing us in the direction of the mathematical Greek genius from 300 BCE, but in the direction of Benedict Spinoza, the Euclid of the Age of Enlightenment!

In his 47th Proposition, Spinoza tells us what lies at the very heart of Freemasonry's teaching — it's all interior work! The answers to everything are inside us. So too is our connection to the essence of God, that imperishable, perfect, unblemished part of us; our true self; the sprig of acacia; our divine spark; our inextinguishable spark of Supreme Consciousness; an imperishable part within us which bears the nearest affinity to the Supreme Intelligence which pervades all nature, and which will never, never, never die.

Says Richard A. Graeter 33° of Spinoza's *Ethics*:

> *It is a work of moral therapy that seeks to liberate the reader from the power of the passions and give us control over our lives. The hope of Ethics is to convert passions into actions, not by repressing human affectivity but by bringing it to a higher level of self-consciousness. In other words, his Ethics lays the foundation for a peculiar system of morality that teaches men to circumscribe their desires and keep their passions within due bounds with all mankind.*[63]

Understand

Spinoza admonished people to use reason to understand the world and each other. Lack of understanding and reason was the cause of man's sadness, which Spinoza wished to remedy.

'The highest activity a human being can attain is learning for understanding, because to understand is to be free', said Spinoza. 'Do not weep; do not wax indignant. Understand. I have striven not to laugh at human actions, not to weep at them, nor to hate them, but to understand them.'

By understanding nature and people, and applying reason rather than emotion or superstition, we can alleviate a lot of the stress in our lives.

'I call him free who is solely led by reason,' said Spinoza. 'True virtue is life under the direction of reason.'

The highest kind of oneness

Spinoza believed that there is only one infinite and eternal reality, and it is prior to all manifested and conditioned existences. All things, and therefore all of mankind, are one in essence. God, Spinoza believed, is not made up of an infinite number of pieces but is one. Everything is contained in the one substance, but nothing is prior to substance. Man embarks on his journey to the knowledge of the union which the mind has with nature. As he arrives at such knowledge, he understands and lives in harmony with the One in the many. The thinking mind, Spinoza believed, tends towards the highest kind of 'oneness' and this oneness is what brings freedom or salvation.

Acquiring this knowledge is no easy task, according to Spinoza, who at the conclusion of *Ethics* writes: 'If the way which, as I have shown, leads hither seems very difficult, it can nevertheless be found. It must indeed be difficult, since it is so seldom discovered; for if salvation lay ready to hand and could be discovered without great labour, how could it be possible that it should be neglected almost by everybody? But all noble things are as difficult as they are rare.'[64]

The same could be said of Freemasonry. Transcending one's base nature, achieving higher consciousness through moral science, igniting one's divine spark and reconnecting with Supreme Consciousness is no easy task, but to use Spinoza's words, 'it can nevertheless be found'. And as Spinoza tells us in his 47th Proposition, the key to finding such knowledge which leads to freedom and salvation is in the human mind, in the brain, which has knowledge of the eternal and infinite essence of God, or Supreme Consciousness.

When we understand the true meaning of the 47th Proposition of Euclid as mentioned in the third degree lecture, we realise what an awesomely beautiful symbol it is in the grand scope of Masonic teaching. It is little wonder that the symbol is used in many countries as that of the Past Master, or one who has symbolically arrived at the realisation of his internal connection to Supreme Consciousness, to God: the highest kind of 'oneness'.

– 24 –
The Past Master

The jewel of the Past Master, he being one who has served as Worshipful Master of a Lodge dispensing Wisdom from the East, is the compasses placed over a quadrant.

A quadrant is 1/4 of a circle, achieved by cutting a circle into four equal parts by means of two lines intersecting each other at the centre, each of the four angles formed at 90°, making them right angles, or square angles. The exact definition of a quadrant is a quarter of a circle made by two radiuses at right angles and the connecting arc.

As defined in our ritual, the quadrant (and thus the square) is the fourth part of a circle. This is important to note. The Masonic quadrant used in the Past Master's jewel is not the first, second or third part of a circle, but the fourth, symbolising the final piece to complete the circle (more on that later).

The compasses are laid over the quadrant, and the quadrant provides proof as to the angle of 60° to which the compasses are opened. Sixty degrees is one-third of an equilateral triangle, the definition of which is a triangle with all three sides of equal length. In the familiar Euclidean, equilateral triangles are also equiangular; that is, all three internal angles are also congruent to each other and are each 60°. They are regular polygons and can therefore also be referred to as regular triangles.

The equilateral triangle

The equilateral triangle represents perfect balance, as all sides are of equal length, and the triangle appears the same from all directions. It therefore teaches that the man who wears this jewel has learned the lessons of Freemasonry and lives a balanced life. It also shows that the wearer of this jewel has served equally in the South as Junior Warden, the West as Senior Warden, and the East as Worshipful Master.

Delving deeper into the symbolism of the equilateral triangle, we find that it represents perfect balance of man:

• Mind/Soul

- Body
- Spirit
  or
- Physical
- Psychological
- Psychical

Writes Mackey[65]:

> *The equilateral triangle appears to have been adopted by nearly all the nations of antiquity as a symbol of the Deity, in some of his forms or emanations, and hence, probably, the prevailing influence of this symbol was carried into the Jewish system, where the Yod within the triangle was made to represent the Tetragrammaton, or sacred name of God.*

The individual journey

The equilateral triangle is representative of our life journey. In alchemical symbolism, it represents the three planes of existence which we experience in our journey of human consciousness: 1. the physical plane (body); 2. the mental plane (mind); 3. the astral plane (spirit).

The three equal sides of the equilateral triangle are also representative of the Masonic journey, from 1. Entered Apprentice to 2. Fellowcraft, and finally being raised to 3. the Sublime Degree of Master Mason. He begins with his birth and emergence from darkness (Entered Apprentice), progresses to his long journey of inner discovery (Fellowcraft), and finally the realisation of his true identity, his Divine Spark, the imperishable part of himself which 'serves to remind us that there is an imperishable part within us which bears the nearest affinity to the Supreme Intelligence which pervades all nature and which will never, never, never die.' At this point the Mason is raised from a symbolic grave, that is, he loses his identity (ego) and is raised in his original, divine consciousness, reconnected with Supreme Consciousness.

The aspiration

Drawn with its point facing up, the equilateral triangle symbolises duality and neutrality. The two lines that diverge from the apex show the two sides of duality – plus and minus, positive and negative, attraction and repulsion – which are united by the horizontal line below.

The upward facing equilateral triangle symbolises our aspiration to transcend the duality of physical life, and achieve a higher consciousness, free of duality. It is the aspiration of the human towards higher unity. Psychologically it represents the urge to escape from duality or the extension represented by the base of the triangle, a movement towards an origin or an irradiating point at the apex.[66]

The Trinity

The three equal sides of the triangle represent will-power, intellect and feeling of the mental world; plus, minus and neutral of the physical world; power, legality and life of the astral world, thus symbolising overall the mind, body and spirit. In the Christian world, the three sides of the triangle represent the Holy Trinity: Father, Son, Holy Spirit; in Hindu religion there is Brahma, Vishnu, Shiva, the creator, the preserver, and the destroyer; for Ancient Egypt Osiris, Isis, Horus; for Greco-Roman belief Zeus, Poseidon, Hades.

Mystic teachings incorporate the power of three, indicated by the equilateral triangle. One represents force; two represents an opening; three represents the birthing of wisdom. The triangle (3) symbolises the union of one and two.

Historic and cultural trinities represented by the equilateral triangle include:

- Waxing moon, Waning moon, Full moon
- Spirit, Mind, Body
- Father, Son, Holy Spirit
- Mother, Father, Child
- Past, Present, Future
- Power, Intellect, Love
- Thought, Feeling, Emotion
- Love, Truth, Wisdom
- Creation, Preservation, Destruction

Pythagoras' Tetractys

Two of the greatest symbols in Pythagorean teaching, the lesser tetractys of ten points, and the greater of thirty-six points, each form an equilateral triangle. Pythagoras called the tetractys a symbol of the musical, arithmetic and geometric ratios upon which the universe is built. The four lines of the tetractys held special meanings for students of the Pythagorean school:

1st line – a single point, the divine dimension from which everything is created.

214 — FREEMASONRY'S HIDDEN BRAIN SCIENCE

2nd line – two points, signifying the first dimension.

3rd line – three points, symbolising the second dimension and harmony, being the marriage of physical beauty and mental balance.

4th line – four points representing the four elements of the ancient world: earth, water, fire, air.

Equilibrium

The balance of the three sides of the equilateral triangle, that is a triangle of 60°+60°+60°, brings about equilibrium in one's earthly life. It also returns us to the number 9, which we visited earlier.

60+60+60 = 180 = 1+8+0 = 9

The quadrant of the Past Master's jewel, being the fourth part of a circle, or, *1-4.* of 360°, equals an angle of 90°, which brings us to 9 as 90 = 9+0 = 9. It should also come as no surprise that the horizontal line of a square, which is an angle of 90°, points us to the East, the place of wisdom, enlightenment and illumination.

That amazing number 9

Let's take another look at the number 9, which as previously detailed becomes apparent in the lodge room when one pays attention to the knocks on the door and the gavel raps of the officers during circumambulation of the candidate for the third degree.

Freemasonry teaches how we can grow and develop as individuals, raising our consciousness towards a reconnection with Supreme Consciousness. Written by geniuses, Masonic ritual imports teachings from various systems of morality and self-improvement, offering several interpretations to its symbols and important numbers.

When exploring the recurring number 9, we can't overlook the Buddhist theory of the Nine Levels of Consciousness. Buddhism teaches that suffering arises from impurities of perception and consciousness. For this reason, purifying the consciousness became a goal of Buddhist practice. The Nine Levels of Consciousness describes the makeup of the conscious and subconscious realms.[67]

The first five of these levels are our senses, in order as such:

1 Sight
2 Hearing
3 Smelling
4 Taste
5 Touch

The sixth level is the Mind.

6. The Mind
This is the level that integrates and processes the information from the five senses into a coherent whole. We spend the majority of our time in these first six levels of consciousness, where our everyday activities take place.

The next level is known as inner looking, or inner self.

7. Inner Looking
This is where we begin to look internally instead of externally. It is at the seventh level of consciousness that we begin to understand the Masonic exhortation: 'The internal not the external qualifications of a man are what Freemasonry regards.'

The next level of consciousness, known as 'ayala', correlates to what modern psychology would call the unconscious mind.

8. The Unconscious Mind
This is the first level of consciousness to survive beyond death of the physical body. This is the level of karma, the level at which all past and present experiences, all good and evil deeds, are stored. It is the level of never-perishing consciousness, and the level at which spiritual phenomena occur. [68]

The final level of consciousness is pure consciousness.

9. Pure Consciousness
Termed the 'amal' consciousness, this level is your true eternal self-existing in harmony with the life of the cosmos itself. Pure consciousness is attained by reaching enlightenment.

Nines everywhere
- The number of consciousness in Greek
- The number of openings in the body (the human body is known as 'the city of nine gates'). They are: two ears, two eyes, two nostrils, the mouth, the urinary opening, and the anus.

Past Master's Jewel

- According to Etchegoyen, 9 is the expression of the power of the Holy Spirit
- St Paul's nine fruits of spirit which are love, joy, peace, patience, kindness, goodness, truthfulness, gentleness and self-control
- 24 hours a day = 1440 minutes = 1+4+4+0 = 9
- Number of Greek muses
- The verb 'to pray' is used 153 times in the OT; 153 = 1+5+3 = 9
- The apostles caught 153 fish in their nets after the appearance of Christ who told them to cast their nets to the right of the boat. 153 = 1+5+3 = 9
- Luke writes that on 14 occasions, Jesus blessed 94 people. 14 + 94 = 108 = 1+ 8 + 0 = 9
- The sun's diameter is 864,000 miles = 8 + 6 + 4 + 0 + 0 + 0 = 18 = 1 + 8 = 9
- The moon's diameter is 2160 miles = 2 + 1 + 6 + 0 = 9
- A circle is 360° = 3 + 6 + 0 = 9
- An equilateral triangle is three angles of 60° = 60 + 60 + 60 = 180 = 1 + 8 = 9
- A square has four angles of 90° = 90 + 90 + 90 + 90 = 360 = 3 + 6 = 9
- A pentagon has five angles of 108° = 108 x 5 = 540 = 5 + 4 + 0 = 9
- A hexagon has six angles of 120° = 120 x 6 = 720 = 7 + 2 + 0 = 9
- When you bisect a circle the resulting angle always reduces to nine converging into a singularity
- The number of years in the Precession of the Equinoxes is 25,920 = 2 + 5 + 9 + 2 + 0 = 18 = 1 + 8 = 9

Completion

In the Bible, the number 9 represents completion of a cycle of growth.

There were nine generations from Adam to Noah, and nine generations from Noah to Abraham.

When Abram received covenant from God, and his new name Abraham, he was 99 years old, which reduces to 9 (9 + 9 = 18 = 1 + 8 = 9), thus representing the period of time in which the spiritual cycle is completed.

A Masonic Past Master is one who has completed all the officers' chairs in the lodge, at last having presided in the Oriental Chair in the East. It is fitting, therefore, that the number 9 is associated with the Past Master, as it represents completion.

Nine is completion of the perfect man in physical state, represented by the equilateral triangle (60+60+60 = 180 = 1+8+0 = 9; mind/soul, body, spirit), and completion of the life cycle, heaven, eternity, the universe, represented by a circle (90+90+90+90 = 360 = 3 + 6 + 0 = 9).

As a circle has no beginning and no end, it is a shape representative of God, or Supreme Consciousness, perfect in all its parts. Wrote Hermes Trismegistus: 'God is a circle whose centre is everywhere and whose circumference is nowhere.'

Circles are used in both the symbols of male and female. They move unrestricted, suggesting energy and power, representing the infinite and unity/oneness – all of which are characteristics of Supreme Consciousness/God/the Universal Mind. Circles protect what's inside their boundaries, they are defence, endurance, safety, femininity and the womb. And how long does it take for the completion of a human from conception to birth? Nine (9) months.

Past Master's quadrant

The quadrant on the Past Master's jewel, being the fourth part of a circle and thus completing the circle, replaces the square worn by the Worshipful Master.

Curved as it is, the quadrant symbolises the curved skull, which houses the brain.

Symbolically, the Past Master, having presided in the East and now permanently residing in the East (where Past Masters sit in the lodge room) has attained knowledge of the brain (higher consciousness) over the body (lower consciousness), which is why the quadrant replaces the square. He has achieved spiritual knowledge over material knowledge, completing the ignition of his Divine Spark, which is his connection with Supreme Consciousness.

The Past Master sits at the left of the Worshipful Master, which is actually at the right side of the brain when viewing the lodge room from its entrance. The right brain is associated with the intuitive, abstract, and creative principle – our higher spiritual nature.

The inner and outer doors of the lodge are situated in the West, the outer door guarded by the Tyler, representing the brain stem. When one enters the lodge through the outer door, he faces East, in the direction of the Worshipful Master, representative of the hypothalamus.

It is important to reiterate that the three principal officers form a triangle within the Lodge room, with the Worshipful Master and Senior Warden opposite one another, and the Junior Warden in the centre. Likewise, in the brain, the hypothalamus (Worshipful Master, East) is situated opposite the pituitary (Senior Warden, West) with the pineal gland (Junior Warden, South) at the midpoint, forming a triangle.

Age of Enlightenment and the genius behind the symbol

The seemingly simple jewel of the Past Master contains deep neurological, numerological, metaphysical and moral lessons, proving again the genius of the Masonic ritual writers.

These men were not shackled by religious dogma. Truly enlightened beings, they were free-thinkers, deep thinkers, incredibly well read and researched in every religion, school, philosophy and subject that offered contribution to the end goal of their development of Freemasonry as we know it today: self-improvement.

These men, who emphasised reason and individualism over tradition, were geniuses-in-excelsis during the Western European 'Age of Enlightenment' of the late 17th and 18th centuries, so called because of the explosion of knowledge, science, and access to those tools that brought forward much of our modern way of thinking. They studied everything from the Cabala to the religious and philosophical systems of the East; the Vedas and the Zend-Avesta; the old Hermetic and alchemical works; the teachings of Pythagoras, and Hermes Trismegistus; the mathematics of Euclid; the philosophical teachings of Aristotle, Confucius, Socrates, Locke, Diogenes, Spinoza, Al-Ghazali; the Egyptian mystery schools, and more. Plumbing the depths of Masonic ritual, it is clear to see the words and symbols tinctured with the lessons of the Jewish Cabala, Hermetic and Rosicrucian teachings, the School of Pythagoras, the principles of Neoplatonism, Buddhist beliefs, Christian influence, numerology, Bruno Giordano's cosmology, Euclidean geometry, and Benedict Spinoza's philosophy, the point of which was 'not just to interpret the world, but to redeem it.'[69] In this regard the work of Freemasonry is the same as that of Spinoza.

The Age of Enlightenment, during which much of our current Masonic ritual was penned, was a time when open-minded thinkers used knowledge to propel forward both themselves and humanity. These enlightened, learned men discovered and taught that we have the tools inside of us to solve our problems and transcend our animal, brute nature. They realised that divinity, a connection to Supreme Consciousness, which provides the ability to transcend, was already inside of them, not outside in the heavens sitting on a great white throne. Deepak Chopra summed it up best when he said: 'I was an atheist until I realised that God was inside of me.'

The progress of the square and compasses from the Entered Apprentice degree to the Fellowcraft degree and the Master Mason degree, and then to the Past Master degree where the square is replaced by the quadrant, is illustrative of the belief of the Masonic ritual writers that the path to enlightenment is not a sudden epiphany, but a gently incremental process.

Freemasonry holds the answers to so many questions about who we are, why we are and what we need to be, but not when interpreted in a literal sense. One must study the words of ritual and the symbols of the Craft from a sense of searching out the clues and uncovering the hidden truths that the many words and symbols conceal.

A secret is only a secret until it is found. Freemasonry will never hand you those secrets gift-wrapped with a pretty ribbon. The prompts and clues are there for all to see, but you must do the groundwork. The Masonic ritual writers did not use Google directness. On the contrary, they embedded their secret wisdom, vouchsafed to them by the great teachers of the mystery schools, in symbols and allegories to be taken as fiction on the surface, but revealing the profoundest truths and knowledge to those who travel deeper.

– 25 –
God and Supreme Consciousness, a synonymity

'Supreme Consciousness' is a term used throughout this book. It is that from which our human consciousness is born, the source to which we aspire to return, and the qualities we desire to acquire.

Your divine spark is your connection to Supreme Consciousness. It is the unblemished, eternal, highest part of yourself that is your piece of God within. It is the sprig of acacia in Masonic ritual, which we are told serves to remind us that there is an imperishable part within us which bears the nearest affinity to the Supreme Intelligence which pervades all nature and which will never, never, never die.

'Consciousness is energy' states the Bhagavad Gita 2.17. 'That which pervades the entire body you should know to be indestructible. No one is able to destroy that imperishable soul.'

Supreme Consciousness is God, which may be difficult for those with a traditional Judeo-Christian upbringing to comprehend. God is not a white-bearded man in flowing robes sitting on a throne amongst the clouds surrounding by harp-strumming angels. God is consciousness; Supreme Consciousness.

God is consciousness

How much do we really know about God? And how much do we know about consciousness? The answer to both questions is very little!

The Bible tells us in no uncertain terms that God is a mystery. Job 11:7-9 writes: 'Can you fathom the mysteries of God? Can you probe the limits of the Almighty? They are higher than the heavens above – what can you do? They are deeper than the depths below – what can you know? Their measure is longer than the earth and wider than the sea.'

The same can be said of consciousness. Can you fathom its mysteries? Can you probe the limits of consciousness?

What can you do?

What can you know?

Corinthians 2:7 tell us: 'The wisdom I proclaim is God's secret wisdom, which is hidden from human beings.'

Consciousness generates intelligence and wisdom.

For centuries man has tried to locate God, perceiving God as an external. But God is not external to us, God is internal. Consciousness is internal. Jesus said: 'The Kingdom of God [Supreme Consciousness] is not something that can be observed [not external; not in a specific location]. The Kingdom of God is within you [consciousness is internal].'

Says the Bhagavad Gita:

He [Supreme Consciousness] *dwells in the world, enveloping all – everywhere.'*

God cannot be measured. There is no size, height, weight, depth or scope of any kind attributed to God. God is outside of time and space. Consciousness too cannot be measured. It has no weight, no height, no depth, no scope. Consciousness is outside of time and space, it is omnipresent and omniscient.

The potential of God is infinite, and we are infinite potential trapped in physical form. Man is capable of great things when he unlocks his potential, and there are no boundaries to the creativity born from his consciousness.

Consciousness is neither male nor female; it is all. Consciousness extends beyond gender. God, too, is all. We are told in Genesis: 'So God [Supreme Consciousness] created mankind [human consciousness placed into matter] in his own image, in the image of God he created them; male and female [the duality of man's nature; man's psychological tendencies] he created them.

I am that I am

Supreme Consciousness has no beginning and no end. The greatest philosophical and scientific minds have tried to define consciousness without success. Supreme Consciousness is the uncaused Cause, the uncreated Creator.

Consciousness is what it is – it just IS! God is what it is, or as God said to Moses, 'I AM THAT I AM.' This is a statement of Absolute Self Awareness. It is the aseity of God; the aseity of Supreme Consciousness.

Your true self is not Michael, John, Christopher, Francis; a bank teller, an insurance broker, a plumber, or a lawyer. Your true self is your divine spark, your direct connection to Supreme Consciousness, which is I AM

THAT I AM. When asked if he is a member of the Royal Arch, considered to be the completion of the Master Mason degree, the Royal Arch Mason answers, 'I am that I am', thus recognising Supreme Consciousness within himself and as himself.

Reads the Workings of the Royal Arch Degree:

> *I AM THAT I AM – the Alpha and Omega – the Beginning and the End – the First and the Last – who WAS, and IS, and IS TO COME – the Almighty. It is the Sacred and Mysterious Name of the actual, future, eternal, unchangeable and all-sufficient God [Supreme Consciousness] who alone has His being in and from Himself and gives to all others their being; so that [Supreme Consciousness] IS what [Supreme Consciousness] WAS, WAS what [Supreme Consciousness] IS, and will remain both WHAT [Supreme Consciousness] WAS and WHAT [Supreme Consciousness] IS from everlasting to everlasting, all creatures being dependent on His [Supreme Consciousness'] mighty will and power.*

In Ephesians 4:6 we're told that there is, 'One God and Father All, who is above all, and through all, and in you all.' This is a description of Supreme Consciousness, which placed consciousness into matter, thus creating us as an extension of itself, and remains above us, through us, and in us.

Corinthians 3:16 tells us that God dwells in us, that is, Supreme Consciousness dwells in us. It is our divine spark, that part of Supreme Consciousness within – the temple not made with hands, eternal in the heavens. This is why Freemasonry focuses on the interior work, as did all ancient mystery schools. Remembering that it is the internal, not the external qualities of a man that Freemasonry regards, the Craft recognises that only by looking inside do we realise that we are not our thoughts, memories, family history, culture, job title, military rank, bank account, physique, or nationality. We are deeper than all of these. We are internalised Supreme Consciousness, the Presence, always watching the activities of the mind/soul, which is composed of consciousness.

God is not coming

Freemasonry is one of many paths for the attainment of higher consciousness, which is the ultimate goal in life. This is why the Candidate for Freemasonry must profess a belief in a higher power, a Supreme Being – Supreme Consciousness – otherwise the teachings are useless. If one doesn't realise a higher power – does not accept that they are a spark of divine energy, an extension of Supreme Consciousness in a physical state – enlightenment is a futile pursuit, as you are within Supreme Consciousness and Supreme Consciousness is within you.

Too often we view God as an external force, thus separating God from ourselves as two distinct entities. But God is within you. Supreme Consciousness is a part of you. It is all internal.

Einstein realised empty space is not really empty. Many great sages, saints, mystics, yogis, and teachers have looked within themselves and realised that within the emptiness is a web of energy and a depth of power which connects all things. It is the Vedic concept of Nada Brahma, and the concept of Logos – the vibratory source that extends through all things, including you. Do not think of God as a noun, that is, as a person, place or thing. Doing so immediately separates you from God/Supreme Consciousness. God is not coming; Supreme Consciousness is already inside you. This is the difference between believing and knowing. Once you know, you can begin the process of igniting your divine spark. As Tony Robbins says: 'Our greatest human adventure is the evolution of consciousness. We are in this life to enlarge the soul, liberate the spirit, and light up the brain.'

This process of illumination, of lighting up the brain, is not for the acquisition of material pleasures, it is the realisation of Raising the Master, or what Hindus call *Sachchidananda*.

In Advaita Vedanta, Sachchidananda is considered a description of the Absolute (Brahman). It translates in three parts: ever-existing eternal truth (Sat); infinite consciousness (Chit); ever new bliss (Ananda).

Change your perception
That which the Western world attributes to God, the Eastern world attributes to consciousness. Why? Because they are one and the same.

God and consciousness are synonymous.

Substitute the word 'God' or 'Father' with the word 'consciousness' and see how your perception changes.

God is creative and creating, and all creation is God.

Consciousness is creative and creating, and all creation is of Consciousness.

God is all-pervading.

Consciousness is all-pervading.

God is, was and always will be.

Consciousness is, was, and always will be.
God is the source of intelligence and wisdom.
Consciousness generates intelligence and wisdom.
Natural order is a result of *God.*
Natural laws are a result of *Consciousness.*
God resides within you.
Consciousness resides within you.
Our *Father* who art in heaven.
Supreme Consciousness who art in a permanent state of ever
    new bliss.

Footnotes

1. Pike, Albert, *Morals & Dogma of the Ancient and Accepted Scottish Rite,* Washington: Supreme Council, 2011, p. 218

2. Cross sectional area of spinal cord at C2 level

3. MacNulty, Kirk, *The Way of the Craftsman,* Central Regalia Ltd, 2002, p. 3

4. MacNulty, Kirk, *The Way of the Craftsman*, Central Regalia Ltd, 2002, Introduction

5. MacNulty, Kirk, *The Way of the Craftsman,* Central Regalia Ltd, 2002, p. 32

6. http://robertgdavis.blogspot.com/2010/04/path-of-esotericists-among-us.html
    date accessed 6/6/2018

7. A Brief Investigation of the Seven Liberal Arts and Sciences – Origins, Masonic Relevance and Applicability in Modern Life, Doric Lodge 316 AF&AM of Ontario, Canada, Committee of Masonic Education, http://brockvillemasons.com/PDF/Liberal%20Arts%20and%20Sciences.pdf
    date accessed 7/1/2017

8. http://en.wikipedia.org/wiki/Jerome_Bruner
    date accessed 10/4/2018

9. Mackey, Albert, *Encyclopedia of Freemasonry and its Kindred Science Vol. 4*, Jazzybee Verlag, 2016, p. 359

10. http://www.cracked.com/photoplasty_875_25-symbols-you-never-noticed-in-everyday-life/ date accessed 30/08/2015

11. Pike, Albert, *Esoterika*, Scottish Rite Research Society, 2005, preface, xvii

12. Beresniak, Daniel, *Symbols of Freemasonry*, Assouline Publishing, 2000, p. 8

13. https://www.virtual-loi.co.uk/Files/1.524853PrinciplesofMasonicRitual.pdf
    date accessed 28/5/18

14. Albert Mackey, Revered Wisdom Freemasonry, Sterling Publishing Co Inc, New York 2010, p7

15. https://www.livescience.com/3505-chemistry-life-human-body.html
    date accessed 2/2/18

16. Farthing, G William, *The Psychology of Consciousness*, Prentice Hall Facsimile Edition, 1991

17. http://www.dadaveda.com/the-supreme-consciousness-is-inside-you/
    date accessed 20/3/2018

18. Pike, A., *Morals & Dogma of the Ancient and Accepted Scottish Rite of Freemasonry,*

Supreme Council of the 33rd Degree for the Southern Jurisdiction of the United States, Charleston, 1871, p 854

19. Hall, Manly P., *The Lost Keys of Freemasonry*, Dover Publications, New York, 1923, p 64

20. Lomas, Robert, *The Secret Science of Masonic Initiation*, San Francisco: Weiser, 2010.

21. Wilmshurst, W.L., *The Meaning of Masonry*, P. Lund, Humphries & Co.; W. Rider & Son: London, 1922, p. 7

22. Wilmshurst, W.L., *The Meaning of Masonry*, P. Lund, Humphries & Co.; W. Rider & Son: London, 1922, p. 185

23. https://www.endocrineweb.com/endocrinology/overview-pituitary-gland
    date accessed 8/4/2018

24. Sumnger, Ged, *Body Intelligence: Creating a New Environment*, Singing Dragon 2 edition, 2009, p. 183

25. www.universal-tao.com date accessed 7/7/2018

26. https://www.greeka.com/cyclades/paros/paros-products/parian-marble.htm
    date accessed 15/9/2017

27. https://www.britannica.com/place/Jordan-River
    date accessed 8/4/2018

28. https://www.tikkun.org/nextgen/exodus-an-allegorical-portrait-of-the-human-mind-in-its-relationship-to-god
    date accessed 2/2/2018

29. https://www.biblestudytools.com/lexicons/hebrew/kjv/machah.html
    date accessed 1/8/2018

30. https://www.bodymindcentering.com/breathing-the-brain-and-bone-marrow/
    date accessed 2/8/2018

31. https://www.faithandhealthconnection.org/god-and-your-brain/
    date accessed 18/3/18

32. https://www.livescience.com/35219-11-effects-of-oxytocin.html
    date accessed 19/3/2018

33. https://www.livescience.com/35219-11-effects-of-oxytocin.html
    date accessed 19/3/2018

34. http://grandlodgeofiowa.org/docs/GeneralMasonicEducation/TheMagicofMasonicRitual.pdf
    date accessed 18/3/18

35. http://www.themasons.org.nz/cdiv/docs/benefitsoffreemasonry.pdf
    date accessed 19/3/2018

36. MacNulty, Kirk, *The Way of the Craftsman,* Central Regalia Ltd, 2002, p. 58

37. http://www.collective-evolution.com/2014/09/27/this-is-the-world-of-quantum-physics-nothing-is-solid-and-everything-is-energy/
    date accessed 1/4/2018

38. https://rcg.org/realtruth/articles/090806-002-science.html
    date accessed 1.2.2018

39. https://patimes.org/stay-brain-stem-part/
    date accessed 10/4/2018

40. http://www.presention.com/mind-body/emotional-health/stress-can-affect-heart-health
    date accessed 10/4/2018

41. https://www.biblica.com/resources/bible-faqs/in-what-language-was-the-bible-first-written/

42. http://www.biblestudy.org/basicart/why-is-new-testament-written-greek.html
    date accessed 11.4.2018

43. Seton, J. *The Pscyhology of the Solar Plexus and Subconscious Minds,* Edward J Clode, New York, 1914, p. 14

44. Dumont, T.Q., *The Solar Plexus or Abdominal Brain,* Advanced Thought Publishing, Chicago, 1920, p.10

45. http://www.themasonictrowel.com/Articles/master_mason/mason_files/the_potential_candidate_should_we_solicit.htm
    date accessed 4/5/2018

46. https://archive.org/stream/sermonescatholic01aelfuoft/sermonescatholic01aelfuoft_djvu.txt
    date accessed 10.4.2018

47. http://www.yetundeodugbesan.com/#!The-Importance-of-Keeping-Good-Company/c1a5s/226F64EC-71B6-41CC-A28B-98B8FBA3EAC9
    date accessed 30/03/2016

48. http://personalexcellence.co/blog/average-of-5-people/
    date accessed 30/03/2016

49. https://en.wikipedia.org/wiki/Hermes_Trismegistus
    date accessed 30/03/2016

50. http://www.forbes.com/sites/rogerdooley/2013/02/26/fake-smile/#57c00245334c
    date accessed 30/03/2016

51. http://www.forbes.com/sites/rogerdooley/2013/02/26/fake-smile/#2d3975b2334c
    date accessed 30/03/2016

52. http://www.theatlantic.com/health/archive/2012/07/study-forcing-a-smile-genuinely-decreases-stress/260513/ date accessed 30/03/2016

53. http://www.masonic-lodge-of-education.com/freemason-symbols.html
    date accessed 5/7/2018

54. Jung, C. *Man and His Symbols,* Dell Publishing Co, USA, 1968

55. http://altreligion.about.com/od/symbols/a/Spirals.htm
    date accessed 3/5/2017

56. http://www.nigms.nih.gov/Education/Pages/Factsheet_CircadianRhythms.aspx
    date accessed 10/3/2018

57. http://www.nigms.nih.gov/Education/Pages/Factsheet_CircadianRhythms.aspx
    date accessed 10/3/2018

58. http://www.exactlywhatistime.com/biological-clock/
    date accessed 10/3/2018

59. http://en.wikipedia.org/wiki/Suprachiasmatic_nucleus
     date accessed 10/3/2018

60. Gensler, Harry J., *Formal Ethics*, Routledge, 1996

61. http://altered-states.net/barry/newsletter463/
     date accessed 15/4/2017

62. https://www.caliburnlodge.org/resources/Documents/Masonic%20Papers/

     Freemasonry%27s%20Peculiar%20System%20of%20Morality%20(LEO).pdf
     date accessed 3/3/2018

63. https://www.caliburnlodge.org/resources/Documents/Masonic%20Papers/

     Freemasonry%27s%20Peculiar%20System%20of%20Morality%20(LEO).pdf
     date accessed 3/3/2018

64. http://home.earthlink.net/~tneff/spinkeys.htm
     date accessed 5/5/2018

65. http://www.masonicdictionary.com/triangle.html
     date accessed 5/5/2018

66. https://theosophytrust.mobi/745-triangle#.Ww5dbS9L28U
     date accessed 30/6/2018

67. http://www.sgi-usa.org/memberresources/study/2018_essentials_part3/docs/eng/06_
     EssentialsExam3_p14-15.pdf
     date accessed 17/6/2018

68. http://operationmeditation.com/discover/levels-of-consciousness-a-buddhist-perspective/
     date accessed 29/6/2018

69. Smith, Steven B., *Spinoza's Book of Life: Freedom and Redemption in the Ethic*s, Yale
     University Press, 2003.